E.I.D.
Entrepreneurial Idiot Disease

6 STEPS TO MAKING A
7 FIGURE NET INCOME
IN ANY ECONOMY

Eliminate Your Fear and Reach Success!

By
TODD BATES
with Joseph & James Bridges

ISBN# 978-0-557-53089-2

Book graphics created by Ryan Leisure.

Editing of book by Brandi Cushing.

Entrepreneurial idiot disease is dedicated to the business owners, entrepreneurs, sales professionals, and those in business who strive to reach their highest level of success.

This book was made possible because 20,000 individuals, businesses, and business owners allowed me to help them. To all of them I would like to say thank you.

To my wife Michelle and my kids Alex and Morgan I am extremely grateful for your help in conquering my own E.I.D in getting this book accomplished. Your support throughout the years has made this book a reality and not just an item on my list.

Table of Contents

Chapter 1 - The Challenge of Being an Entrepreneur

Have you ever considered owning your own business or do you already own one?

Running your own company may be one of the most rewarding and challenging experiences that anyone can undertake.

As an entrepreneur you tackle problems that make large corporations run to the government seeking bailout money. For the entrepreneur who "isn't too big to fail" we dig, scrap, and fight for our survival and our livelihood.

There are always challenges standing in the way of success and this is the challenge of the entrepreneur.

Can you get over the hurdles that stand in your way to achieve your definition of success?

Many will try yet not everyone will succeed at their attempts.

Over the last 20 years I have guided business owners, sales people, and entrepreneurs to reach their goals. While helping over 15,000 small business owners, over the last 20 years, I discovered a pattern. The pattern recently revealed itself to me while I was looking at the top 10% of my clients and thinking about why they were successful in comparison to the 90% who hadn't reached the level of success they desired.

This book is going to lay a foundation for you to be successful. Regardless of the economy, your market, or your business model, you will discover how you can achieve the level of success that you have desired yet to this point have been unable to attain.

It doesn't even matter where you are right now. If you bought this book to start your first business, or your business is doing over 15 million a year in sales, you will find the tools, models, and strategies necessary to get you to the next level.

Most of all I am happy that you took on the challenge of being an entrepreneur. Welcome to the fight for success!

The Disease Preventing Entrepreneurs From Succeeding

For years I have had a disease that really only my wife and kids knew about. They weren't quite sure what it was, but they knew the symptoms well.

They saw me working at all hours of the day, facing countless challenges, and always meeting other entrepreneurs who were just like me.

Over the last 10 years I have been a Dr of sorts. Some of my clients even call me Dr. Todd. The disease that I diagnosed my clients with is E.I.D. Entrepreneurial Idiot disease. E.I.D. prevents otherwise successful business owners from reaching their true potential.

Fortunately I have seen even the worst cases of this disease cured by the steps I am going to reveal to you over the course of this book. Many of the cases of E.I.D. that I have observed have been thought hopeless by others. However, the cure exists and you have taken the first step to recovery by reading this book.

20 Years in the Entrepreneurial Trenches

Some say entrepreneurs are born not made. I believe that you can become an entrepreneur with the right mind set, as I have been doing for the past 20 years.

My background comes from starting immediately out of college in the entrepreneurial world. College taught me the principle of seeing something all the way through, yet I realized early on that I was not going to show up to a 9 to 5 job and be told what to do.

Success is attainable provided you are willing to pay the price. When I left college I had no choice but to succeed. I was over $80,000 in debt, without a single family member that was able to lend me a dime.

Early on I realized you have put yourself in a position where success is the only option.

I have made over $1 million annually every year since I was 23. Throughout this book, I will reveal in extreme detail how you can re-create my success, just like countless numbers of my clients in my "Success Circle" have.

A client of mine asked me recently why I didn't call my "Success Circle" a millionaire club, and the reason is simple. Success is defined by each one of us and not by the outside world. The outside world may only value money, yet I encourage you to find your own true definition of success.

One of the members of my "Success Circle" makes less than $75,000 annually, yet works less than 3 days a week, never misses one of his children's activities, and lives debt free. Could he have a bigger business? Yes. Does he want a bigger company at this time? At the moment he is content having met his goal for success. Meeting your own personal goal for success is the real American dream.

Currently I operate 47 different companies. Each one of them serves a different niche, market, and customer base. Some of these companies I operate with clients of mine and others are projects that I have been interested in since I decided to become and entrepreneur.

Entrepreneurs often get bored very quickly and I am no different. The variety of companies I own give me something new, exciting, and most of all different to do on a near daily basis.

How To Get the Most Out Of This Book

Wherever you are in your entrepreneurial journey this book has been designed to help you get to the next level.

There are 6 steps to becoming a successful entrepreneur. At any time you can skip to a chapter that matches one of the issues you are facing in your business.

Entrepreneurs, like me, often have issues focusing on one topic for a length of time and as such I would encourage you to take advantage of how this book has been designed to get you to the next level quickly.

As you address the issues in your business feel free to come back and tackle another chapter. Working through the six steps in this book will put you on the path to success.

Chapter 2 – The Biggest Problems Facing Entrepreneurs Today

Being an entrepreneur means having the confidence to work without a safety net. You are out there on your own day to day battling for new sales, new accounts, and new clients. This presents challenges that many who work in the corporate world can't comprehend.

In the corporate world they can blame the economy, financing, competition, or a "new law" as to why they aren't hitting the sales goals that they need to turn a profit.

When an economy gets tough some entrepreneurs adopt attitudes similar to the following:

- The economy is bad
- My competition came up with a new product
- The law changed
- It is hard to get financing

One trait that my clients have always been able to count on from me is a very direct and to the point answer to their question.

How do I make money regardless of economic conditions and what my competition is doing?

Let me be very clear about where you are in your entrepreneurial journey:

It's your fault.

Good or bad it is your fault. You are responsible for your success or your failure. The sooner you can take responsibility for where you are, the faster you can reach your next goal.

Before you start providing excuses, you can be sure that I have heard every excuse that exists. Everyone has different problems or issues they are facing, and realizing that you are solely responsible allows you to remove the excuses and start making progress on a solution.

Allow me to share a story that will illustrate the kind of problems entrepreneurs face.

A few years ago a client lost her home to a fire. Her insurance failed to cover all of the necessary expenses to rebuild her home. She could have taken the attitude of "it's not my fault this happened and I should not have to fix this." Instead, she chose to adopt the attitude of, "this is my home and it's my responsibility to fix it".

In one year she went from being in the hole over $200,000 to making $700,000. If she had blamed the insurance company, the universe, and everyone else she never would have reached her goals.

Understanding Who You Are

Have you ever watched professional sports?

Professional athletes spend their time doing the one thing that they do best for their sport. One of the sports where athletes specialize is football. Football is made up of specialists and each one has to do their job so the team wins. One of the specialists that gets little credit yet is critical to the game is the place kicker.

Kickers are called out only in the most specific situations. They don't try and pass for touchdowns, rush for 150 yards, or catch passes. They stay focused on the one thing they do best and leave the rest to other specialists.

Entrepreneurs who specialize are the most successful because they are focused on what they do best.

There are two questions that every entrepreneur has to ask to get to the next level. These questions are as follows:

- What am I the best at?
- What am I the worst at?

The answers to these questions will change the course of your business. Each answer will provide more time for you to generate more sales in your business.

Over the course of this book we will spend time looking at the 6 steps or areas where you need to have answers to these questions.

Entrepreneurs

America was built on an adventurous spirit. This spirit is alive and well today in entrepreneurs. Everything that we have has been created by brave souls who chose to go it on their own and forage ahead creating and fulfilling a need in a market.

Corporate America does not create, they maintain, which leaves room for the entrepreneur to find a niche and grow their product and company.

Let's look into a few more traits often found in entrepreneurs. The goal of overcoming E.I.D. is to bring these traits to the surface so your success is all but guaranteed.

Why being an entrepreneur is the greatest career choice available today

One important point that I enjoy sharing with fellow entrepreneurs is the need to design your own destiny. I am not talking about reading a crystal ball or guessing, I am speaking of having a clear picture of what the future looks like for the entrepreneurs company.

During a recent 1 on 1 conversation with one of my consulting clients I asked them the question that I ask every client, and I invite you to ask yourself right now:

"What does your business look like 5 years from now?

This particular client of mine was able to share in extreme detail their vision for their company. The detail in which entrepreneurs describe their vision always amazes me. They can tell me the number of staff they are going to have, the impact they are going to make in the community, where they will be located, and how their product will be received by the market.

While income eventually comes up during these talks most entrepreneurs don't start their companies with an income goal in mind. Later I will discuss how this is part of E.I.D. and how to solve it. For now I would like you to get clear on your vision of what your company looks like and what you want it to be.

The process of taking a concept and building an entire company is one that true entrepreneurs love. It is the reason I have 47 different companies that I operate. The process of starting something new, and bringing it from a simple idea to a company that generates sales, is addicting.

99% of entrepreneurs are serial entrepreneurs. They are always thinking of the next idea, next product, and while this leads to E.I.D. it is also what makes them great and their companies great as well.

For those of you who are familiar with the comic strip Dilbert, you know his tales of the corporate world. The comics are always entertaining, yet difficult for me to relate to as I never spent a single minute in a corporate cubical.

Many of my clients have spent not only minutes but years of their lives in corporate America and the thought of going back is enough to keep them moving forward. Two partners and I have launched several companies. They have shared their tales from corporate America with me. They tell me about how they spent more time filling out reports on what they were doing, rather than actually doing the work, because that is what their bosses instructed them to do. When I hear these stories, it amazes me that many of the largest companies in the world ever turn a profit.

Entrepreneurs want to get out and enjoy life. Their goal is to build a company that gives them the freedom they didn't have in their previous corporate life. Most entrepreneurs find the freedom they desire, but not the income they desire. This is a key symptom of E.I.D. Freedom of time, freedom of choice, and freedom to take action are what they seek and this adds to their success.

E.I.D is the primary "disease" this book will reveal to you and how to conquer it. One of the additional "diseases" I would like to bring to your attention is BDD (Business Deficit Disorder). You may be suffering from it now, until you start another company.

These are some of the good and bad traits entrepreneurs all have in common. However, I like to think of it solely in the good category. Entrepreneurs love solving problems and sometimes when they have severe BDD they may have 6 companies (or 47) going at the same time. Provided you get through the 6 steps I am going to be sharing with you, having BDD will not threaten your business.

One last trait that entrepreneurs have in common, and the one that leads them to success, is they are all "people persons". They are great with their customers. This is why 99% of my clients have customers who just love them and why they always manage to pay the bills. The goal is to get beyond just paying the bills.   However, this core trait of being good with people is critical to the success of the entrepreneur.

There are two types of entrepreneurs and they face off on a regular basis. The two kinds of entrepreneurs are:

Jumpers vs. Thinkers

Jumpers vs. Thinkers and Why Jumpers Will Always Win

The rubber meets the road at every live event when I look to divide the audience between jumpers and thinkers.

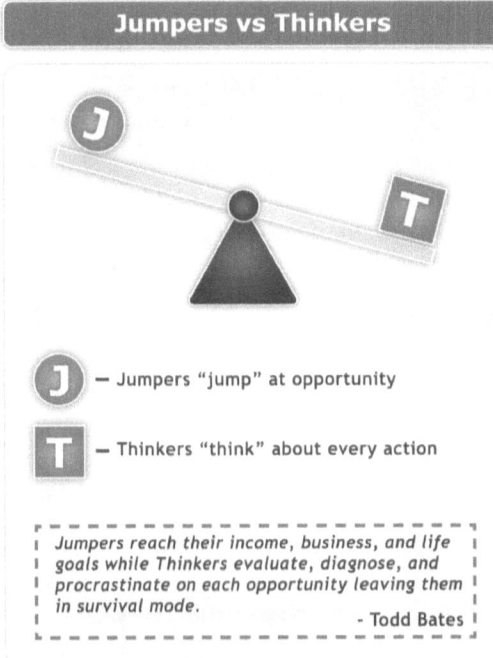

Jumpers vs Thinkers

J — Jumpers "jump" at opportunity

T — Thinkers "think" about every action

Jumpers reach their income, business, and life goals while Thinkers evaluate, diagnose, and procrastinate on each opportunity leaving them in survival mode.

- Todd Bates

At every event I divide the audience into two groups, whether there are 30 or 300 people in the seminar, finding out who is a jumper and who is a thinker is critical to reaching them at their core.

Although you may have guessed by now what these terms mean, let me define them so we are all on the same page.

Jumpers

These entrepreneurs are ready and willing to try something new to increase or improve their business. They leap first and figure out how to make it work after they have made the decision. The decisions they make for their business are swift.

Jumper's biggest hurdle is that they keep jumping at new things before they have finished their last endeavor. This is an EID trait that can be overcome. Jumpers always figure things out in the end because they have no other choice.

Thinkers

This one should be pretty self explanatory. Thinkers think about what they should do. When presented with an opportunity, even if it is 100% guaranteed, they still must take time to think about it.

Their business continues to crawl along barely getting by as they "evaluate" each opportunity that comes across their desk. They suffer from paralysis by analysis. 6 months after an opportunity is presented to them they are still "thinking" about it.

These entrepreneurs run a business that will struggle to grow for years. When, if ever, they take a new opportunity they are nervous, scared, and worry most of the time. Often they will cause projects to fail because they over think them.

Discover Entrepreneurial Marriages & How They Affect Your Business

At my events, I always ask who has business partner. This is always a very interesting conversation. The part of the conversation that is most important is finding out what each of the partners view as their responsibilities.

The optimum entrepreneurial marriage is between a jumper and a thinker. Of course this only works when each partner is treated equally. Jumpers and jumpers work well together also. However, sometimes they are each jumping at different opportunities that take the company resources in different directions.

When two thinkers get together their business will probably move at the speed of an ice berg.

Which one of these are you?

Not everyone is a jumper or thinker 100% of the time. Sometimes you may be one or the other depending on the situation.

One of my clients came to me after having some recent success. At the time, she was willing to jump at every opportunity. I had to talk her out of jumping at everything and find the one opportunity that was best for her company's growth.

Entrepreneurs who are having financial problems may sometimes lean too far to the thinking mode which only makes things worse for them and prevents them from getting to the next level.

Part of E.I.D. management, (you will never be 100% cured), is discovering how to manage these parts of your personality successfully in order to grow your business.

Discover the One Common Trait That E.I.D Entrepreneurs Share

When you have E.I.D. you survive completely off personality. Surviving off personality for an entrepreneur seems great initially. Eventually you discover personality marketing is limited.

Entrepreneurs have the ability to be completely personality based and still manage to generate sales for their business. Many entrepreneurs view this as an asset and it can be yet it eventually turns into a liability as you may already be aware.

The issue with depending on personality is that it depends on the entrepreneur and they can't replicate themselves. They don't have systems in place, so their business is always limited by the extent of their personality and the limits it imposes on their business.

This can be used to the advantage of the entrepreneur and I will walk you through how to make this happen for your business.

E.I.D Entrepreneurs Struggles That Prevent Them from Reaching Success

Every entrepreneur suffering from E.I.D. struggles with a few common traits that I would like to share with you. Overcoming these is a process and won't happen overnight. Identifying which of these traits you have will make curing the disease easier.

My clients who have the worst cases of E.I.D suffer from multiple symptoms. Let's look at a few of the symptoms.

E.I.D. entrepreneurs have the following in common:

- 15 ideas going around in their head constantly and they can't really decided on which one they should focus on.
- They are surrounded by 80% projects. In other words, projects are constantly being started and yet not 100% complete. Jumping at new opportunities is fun and exciting and they just never get around to finishing what they started.
- Not doing $1,000 an hour work. Each business has work that can and should only be done by the entrepreneur who owns the company. This work is $1,000 an hour work, yet having EID means you avoid this work. You may not be intentionally avoiding the $1,000 work which is why you suffer from EID.

The Perfect Business Model That Every Entrepreneur Should Adopt Immediately

Over the years I have helped business owners from just about every sector of business that you can imagine.

The business model that I have always loved the most is the Dr's office. I recommend to all of my clients to model their business after the Dr's office. Allow me to explain why.

In a Dr's office who does 95% of the work?

The head nurse does 95% of the work and the Dr. only comes in to ask a few questions and write the prescription for the pills. In this model, the Dr. is well respected and highly paid. This works because they have a great head nurse.

Ask yourself the following question:

In your business are you the Dr. or the head nurse?

With every coaching client and at every event, I ask my participants to answer this question for themselves. Before they answer, I check to make sure we all know who gets paid the most between the Dr. and the head nurse. The answer is of course the Dr.

To get to the next level, every entrepreneur must turn themselves into the Dr. and get themselves a great head nurse. The nurse does not have to be a full time employee. The head nurse may be software, a system, or even a part time employee. However the point is clear, be the Dr.

Are you headed in the right direction to make your business a success?

Another sign of E.I.D. is when you are heading east looking for a sunset. For those who aren't geographically aware, the sun sets in west. In other words your business is heading in the wrong direction.

Many entrepreneurs aren't even aware that they are heading in the wrong direction. This usually happens because they aren't focused on the right direction for their company.

This is a true sign of EID and one that has to be solved.

6 Signs of E.I.D

As I mentioned earlier, the one trait that my friends, my family, and my clients can count on me for is being direct and to the point.

You are an entrepreneurial idiot if you can't get out of your own way with these 6 traits. One of these may be holding you back more than the others. However, even facing one of them means you suffer from EID.

Throughout the course of this book I will cover in extreme detail these traits and most importantly how to conquer them in your business. Let's look at the signs of EID briefly so we can be prepared for the journey we are about to undertake.

Fear Management

Everyone has fears that prevent them from reaching their true potential. Managing these fears can become a near daily process. Identifying the fears that are holding you back and realizing the need to face them head on will help put you on the path to success.

99% of entrepreneurs have a fear they are unwilling to admit. Until entrepreneurs are willing to admit their fears they will struggle in reaching their goals. We will get to the root of fear management in this chapter.

Marketing

For the last 20 years this has been one of my favorite topics to discuss with my clients. Whether you aren't marketing your business at all, are doing the wrong kind of marketing, or aren't using the right medium, you will struggle for success. Proper marketing is absolutely critical for success.

My belief has long been that if you don't have marketing in your business you don't have a business. In this chapter we will discover how to get your business to the next level through the power of marketing.

Time Management

Have you ever said to yourself "If I only had more time?"

Entrepreneurs are in a constant struggle with the clock. They never have enough time in the day, week, month or even the year. Discovering the secrets behind successful time management will give you the time you need to reach your goals.

Sales & Conversion

Generating leads for your business is part of the equation and the other half is turning those leads into sales.

There is an art and a science behind sales conversion. After having worked with clients in dozens of different industries I will share specifically how to turn a prospect into a client.

From the first call to the final sale converting these leads, which you are spending your hard earned money to get, will be covered.

Goal Setting

Most entrepreneurs set goals, yet most never achieve them. Why?

Usually it comes down to the goal setting process that entrepreneurs undertake. In this chapter I will share with you how I have set goals and reached them 98% of the time successfully. My clients who set goals following this goal setting method have twice as much income as those who do not set goals.

Money Management

Have you ever made money and wondered "where did it all go"?

Money management for entrepreneurs is critical to the long term success of your business. Managing your money the entrepreneurial way can set you up for a lifetime of success.

In this chapter I will uncover all of the bad money traits that entrepreneurs share and how to overcome them for success.

Weakest Link

The phrase "you are only as strong as your weakest link" applies directly to EID. In the EID traits I covered above, finding and addressing your weakest link is critical to your success. If one of the above traits jumped out at you please feel free to skip to that chapter so you can be on your way to managing your EID.

Chapter 3 - How to Prevent the #1 Cause of Business Failure by Discovering How an Entrepreneur Can Manage the Fear that is Crippling Their Business

Overcome Your Fears and Get Yourself to the Next Level

After coaching over 20,000 clients, one on one, I can tell you that the number 1 item that prevents entrepreneurs from achieving success is Fear. As you are starting this chapter I am going to challenge you to be very honest with yourself. Be honest enough to understand that we all suffer from fears.

One of the most crippling items for an entrepreneur is to think that they have no fear. You might have achieved some success, have a 7 figure business, and then think "I have made it". After all you have beaten the economy, your customers love you, sales are soaring, so what is there to be afraid of?

This is the same thinking that got the Titanic in trouble. The Titanic was the largest, most beautiful, and powerful ship. Why would they have to scan the horizon for trouble, right? Unfortunately for them they didn't acknowledge the very real fear that an iceberg could be dangerous. Even for the grandest of ships an iceberg still proved deadly, just when they thought there was nothing to fear.

As an entrepreneur, when you can acknowledge your fear, understand it, and then overcome it, you will be able to get your business to the next level. Don't let those people around you say benign statements like "be fearless" or have "no fear". I can tell you that anyone who comes up to you and states "I have no fears" is one of the most fearful people in the room. What I want to challenge you to consider is that regardless of your sales, your bank account, or your success, fear is real.

How to Overcome the Daily Fear That Is Killing Your Business

Fear prevents you from achieving the level of success in your business that you deserve. Most entrepreneurs suffer from fear on a daily basis. To be cured of entrepreneurial idiot disease there isn't a magic "no fear" pill. Entrepreneurial Idiots discover how to acknowledge their fear, manage their fear, and then overcome it.

Let me be direct with you, this is not the fear that is portrayed in movies. It's not a fear of the dark, or walking down an alley wondering what will happen to you. The fears that entrepreneurs face are much different, but just like in the movies, most fears are unfounded. They are created in your mind and act as an anchor that prevents you from success.

One of the first steps on the road to fear management is acknowledging your fear. I acknowledge fear, in my office, on a white board. I have the word fear written out in capital letters like the following:

FEAR

I would challenge you to write it out the same way in your office. This ugly 4 letter word won't stop you when you realize what the definition is. I invite you to define it as follows:

False Evidence Appearing Real

Fears are generally unfounded. The perception is often far worse than the reality. A major challenge occurs in business when we let the false perception become our reality. That false perception can send you in a terrifying downward spiral when left unchecked.

I have found that there are really five major fears that prevent entrepreneurs from success. These five fears have been repeated in many different industries, across many different types of people. Thankfully, there is a cure for each one and knowing them will get you closer to the next level. The five fears are:

1. Fear of What Other People Think Of You
2. Fear of Success
3. Fear of Rejection
4. Fear of Going Broke
5. Fear of the Telephone

You might identify with one fear and you might identify with a few of them. If you can't identify with any of them, read them again! Your fear is in there somewhere and coming to the realization that your fear is real will help you to move forward.

What Do You Think Your Biggest Fear Is?

The first step to overcoming your fear is to identify which one is the toughest for you. In this exercise there is no right or wrong answer. It simply comes down to choosing which one is the biggest challenge for you. With your fear firmly identified, let's go through each fear to discover how you can overcome them.

Don't skip to the fear that you immediately identified. Take time to go through each one. Throughout the life of your business, you will find that different fears will challenge you at different stages of your business. I have each of them written on my board to remind me that there isn't a single fear that could stop me. I want you, just as I am, to be aware of each one.

Fear of What Other People Would Think About You

This is a tough one for many entrepreneurs to embrace. I want you to ask yourself, what would happen if you started making $500,000 a year? What would people start to think about you if you were making $100,000 a month?

It's a question that I often ask attendees of my seminars. I pose the question "do you think you have more friends or fewer friends when you start making a million dollars a year?" Inevitably someone raises their hands and says "more friends".

Wrong!

As you make more money your friends will change. If you can't get over that to begin with, you won't reach the highest levels of your business.

Fear of Rejection & How to Solve It Forever

This is one of the most prevalent fears across any industry. After all, when you are out there trying to sell your product or service and someone says "no", how do you feel? You might feel that they didn't just reject your offering, but they rejected you! This type of negative experience can prevent you from going out the next day (or even in the next hour) and giving your business 100% of your efforts,

I want you to consider the world of medicine when you suffer from the fear of rejection. Envision going into a Doctor's office after waiting for an hour. As you wait patiently in the exam room, the Doctor comes in, barely acknowledging you and then launches into an arsenal of questions. He peppers you with questions for a few minutes, writes some notes down, and then leaves the room.

Doctors never get rejected. They aren't worried about you rejecting them, because they are the expert! They are there to determine what your ailment is and prescribe a solution. Doctors never get rejected because they never make a statement. They only ask questions.

You can do the same in the business world. When you suffer from the fear of rejection, I challenge you to stop answering questions and only ask them. As you become the Doctor, you will notice a transformation. No longer will you fear rejection because you will understand you are the expert, you get to ask the questions, and anyone who doesn't answer your questions better head back to the waiting room.

Fear of Going Broke & Why Even If You Are Broke You Still Have Hope

Regardless of economic conditions this fear plagues many business owners. In tough economies, the news media makes this fear appear more real by sharing "doom and gloom" stories. Besides not listening to the news, I want you to step out on a limb.

Many people come up and tell me "Todd, I am down to my last $1,000" or "Todd, I don't know how I am going to pay my mortgage next month". What I want you to realize is that every entrepreneur who has made it has gone through this fear. To get through this fear, through this disease, you are going to have to risk your credit cards, risk your credit rating, and even risk the equity in your house. If you don't step out on a limb and risk a little bit you aren't paying a big enough price for success.

Fear of the Telephone & How to Conquer It

You won't make it to the next level when you have the fear of talking to strangers. Many entrepreneurs have such large networks of people they know, they never step outside their core group of contacts. While this might sound pleasant, this will keep you stuck in survival mode.

Having the fear of the telephone prevents you from doing heavy money making activity of prospecting. The fear of the telephone is closely associated with the fear of rejection. People view talking to strangers as the chance to get rejected. Get over the fear of the phone by acknowledging that unless you want to be trapped in survival mode, growing your business will require talking to strangers.

Fear of Success May Be the Biggest Fear Entrepreneurs Face

What is your definition of success? I want you to come up with a number that you could make annually that would make you say to yourself that you are successful. I asked one of my clients what her definition of success would be for her business and she told me 1 million.

She told me the number with a huge amount of confidence. I waited a few seconds and I asked her to triple it. Her reaction immediately changed and she proceeded to tell me a myriad of excuses of why that wasn't possible. She told me she wouldn't have enough time, she wouldn't be able to see her family, she would have to get more employees and on and on.

With her immediate reaction, what do you think her chances would be to hit the goal of 3 million? Not likely, until I helped her understand that tripling the business didn't count entirely on her. To overcome the fear of success, I would invite you to consider that you can have systems and people to do the heavy lifting for you. Most people's fear of success is founded on the belief that they will have to do it all, and that keeps them from reaching their real level of achievement.

Identifying Fears Is Just the Beginning To Solving Your E.I.D.

Identifying and acknowledging what fears you have is just the start. It's time to stop letting entrepreneurial idiot disease control your fear. You have the power to manage your fear, and when you do, you will be able to get to the next level.

What is Stopping the Typical Entrepreneurial Idiot

Fear is a complex part of the human brain. Even understanding the definition as merely," False Evidence Appearing Real," is not enough to give you the tools to master your fear. It would be great if we could just identify your core fears in business, wave a magic wand, and say get over it, but that isn't reality. Pumping yourself up or telling yourself to "have no fear" won't help you achieve the level of success you desire, it will likely only help you for a day or two at best.

There are three challenges that I have found that stop the typical entrepreneur. When you can master these challenges, you will be well on your way to the daily management of your fear. The better you manage your fear, the more success you will achieve.

Self Limiting Beliefs That Prevent Entrepreneurs from Achieving Success

The first and one of the most challenging is self limiting beliefs. Self limiting beliefs come down to what you think you can or can't do. For business owners, sales professionals, and entrepreneurs, this can be a deadly thought process that can leave you constantly struggling when left unchecked.

One of the tasks I give attendees of my seminars, to help them see the complexity of this belief, is to add up their monthly bills. I tell them to write all their bills down and put a total on the left side of their paper. After a few minutes I ask them, "How much income are you making right now?"

Usually about 90% of the room answers they are making just enough to pay their bills! They have built their businesses around their bill structure and have limited themselves to making just this amount of money.

The reality is that entrepreneurs always find a way to pay their bills. Entrepreneurial idiots always find a way to pay their car payment, mortgage payment, and go on vacation. Every month you find the amount of money you need to meet your current obligations.

You haven't got it into your head that you can make $30,000 a month, $50,000 a month or even $150,000 monthly. You might not have even considered how your business could generate

$25 million annually in income. This is a self limiting belief! The question then becomes, what are you limiting yourself to?

How Linking the Wrong Belief to Success Can Be Deadly to Your Business

The second item that entrepreneurial idiots do when it comes to fear management is linking the wrong items to success. Before sharing with you how this impacts your world, I want to share an example outside of the business world.

The challenge is to lose 15 lbs. I want you to put it into your mind to lose 15 lbs. With demanding schedules, family lives, etc, we can all afford to lose 15 lbs. What is your immediate reaction to that goal? What is the first thing that comes to mind?

Most Entrepreneurial Idiots think: "great I have to diet", "I have to starve myself", or "I have to work out like 8 days a week"! These are what they are linking to their goals. What do you think the odds are of someone losing 15lbs are if they think they have to "starve", "crash diet" or "workout 8 days a week"? Not likely!

In the business world this same type of poor linking occurs. If you asked most entrepreneurial idiots to make $100,000 a month they would give you a laundry list of excuses. I do ask entrepreneurs, who attend my events the question about making $100,000 a month, and they usually share beliefs with me like; I would have to work 26 hours a day, I would never see my family, etc. Until I can help them change that link, they won't ever make the type of income that they really desire.

Now ask yourself, what are you linking to your goals? If you don't have the right link you will NEVER get to the next level in your business.

One of the easiest methods I have found to quickly identify the beliefs you are linking to your goals is an exercise that I share at my live events. I want you to write down your top three to five goals and what you link to those goals. Don't continue to read on until you have done that. Understanding what you are linking to your goals is a powerful step in breaking through your current ceiling of achievement.

Most Entrepreneurs Are Afraid of Being Exposed of Who They Are

This comes down to reconciling the person people think you are and the person who you really are. Getting this one correct is absolutely essential to fear management. Let me share with you an example from my own life to help illustrate this point.

The Todd Bates person that many people know is the guy who flies around the country, performs 200+ events annually, is outgoing, over the top, extroverted, and very loud. This is the person that my clients and people who have attended my seminars know me as.

Now, the person I really am is a private person. I don't need a lot of friends or feel the need go to endless parties. I am actually OK being alone most of the time.

Most entrepreneurs haven't reconciled this difference within themselves. They don't want people to know their true personality. When you can understand your true person, you will be able to overcome your fears and be who you need to be.

The more you come to know about yourself, the more successful you will be come.

I can't emphasize this point enough. Many people struggle for years, sometimes decades, trying to be everything for everyone. Most entrepreneurs get into this habit because they want to make everyone happy. Trying to make everyone happy all the time will ultimately make your business suffer. I give you permission to realize your true person as that will unlock your potential to achieving success.

Taking time to identify what challenge, or even challenges that you most closely identify with, will help you better manage your fear. Simply knowing if you have been trapped by self limiting beliefs, poor linking, or being afraid of being exposed is not enough. Fear management doesn't happen by simply identification, it happens through change.

Fear Management Requires Change and Change Isn't Easy For Many Entrepreneurs

Entrepreneurs are a crazy bunch. They jump head first into many situations and they run scared from others. Many times the situations that entrepreneurs run scared from are the very ones they need to embrace to reach their income goals. Entrepreneurial Idiot Disease causes entrepreneurs to make flawed decisions.

The good news is that the disease is curable, not an instant pill cure, but curable. One of the first steps to realize is that curing the disease and mastering fear management requires change. Let's be honest, people don't like change. People pay incredible amounts for "quick fixes" because they don't want to put in any effort and they want to see a difference. They want to see a difference in their lives and businesses, all without lifting a finger.

I am asking you to make change by embracing it and understanding it will take some effort. I want you to take the steps of identifying your E.I.D. behavior and then change it! No waiting around, no starting tomorrow, starting now. For many entrepreneurs change can be considered a 4 letter word. It's ugly, it's painful, and should be avoided at all costs. I want you to know that you won't get your business to the next level if you don't accept that change is inevitable.

You may be thinking about putting this book down and getting online to try to find an instant answer to avoid changing. I want you to think about a hurricane. A hurricane is a turbulent force with wind speeds that can exceed 200 mph. It destroys many structures in its path, yet some buildings stand tall and don't fall down. They may bend, but they don't break. Just like the buildings that remain standing in a hurricane, I encourage you to stand strong. Don't go along with the hurricane like everyone else and try to justify it, simply stand tall.

The reality is that everything is always changing. Entrepreneurial idiots don't like admitting that change happens and quite honestly they avoid change at all costs. They don't want to change their self limiting beliefs. They don't want to change their links and they don't want to reveal who they really are.

Get the Cure to E.I.D. Fear Management & Discover How to Be a Smart Entrepreneur

Being a smart entrepreneur doesn't mean going back to school for another degree. The most successful entrepreneurs I know would openly admit that they are "total idiots". They are successful because they have the right mindset. They have discovered how to manage their fear on a daily basis.

Managing your fear and being a smart entrepreneur can be broken down into three parts. Many days you will need to go through all three parts to cure your disease and that's ok. As you have become aware of the challenges and have faced your fears, you are ready to step forward for the cure.

Don't Suffer from Rationalization
This is a deal killer! Many entrepreneurs have such an ingrained habit of rationalization that they don't even realize they do it. In order to overcome rationalization, I want you to recognize the thought process and see how it creeps into your mind.

You can recognize rationalization coming on when you start to feel fear. It could be the fear of rejection, fear of success, fear of going broke, or any other fear, just recognize when you feel it coming into your mind. After you start feeling fear, you will start talking to yourself, probably not out loud. You will start saying things like "I'm not selling because it's not the season" or "I'm not hitting my goals because of the economy". Entrepreneurial idiots rationalize more than anyone else.

Entrepreneurial idiots try to blame things outside of their control. They blame people, economic conditions, anything that prevents them from having to take responsibility. When you start to feel a fear, don't rationalize it, simply recognize it and remember that it is merely False Evidence Appearing Real.

Acknowledging Your Own Success Leads to Breakthroughs for Entrepreneurs

Acknowledging your success can be a tough one because inherently entrepreneurs are overly critical of themselves and their businesses. I don't want you to think about this as a monthly or quarterly task. I want you to recognize your success on a daily basis. Create a reward system for yourself to help you continue the habit.

One of my clients came to me and her goal was to make more money. Now, she suffered from what 99% of entrepreneurs suffer from, she wasn't prospecting enough. I told her that she needed to prospect for at least two hours a day. Each day that she achieved that goal she was to reward herself. Most people stop because they don't see results soon enough. Creating a reward system keeps the positive behavior going until you start to see the financial rewards.

When you acknowledge your success you will have a startling revelation. You will realize that success has nothing to do with luck. Counting on luck or timing isn't a business strategy. It is just a false hope. By recognizing your success on a daily basis you will quickly see that a good month is your fault. You will also see that a bad month is your fault! Embracing this mindset is an essential part of the cure for EID and for managing fear.

Wake Up Daily and Asking One Question that Will Forever Change Your Business

There is no more revealing word for an entrepreneur than the word "how". When you wake up in the morning, before you start your money making activities, I challenge you to think of just one "how" question. It gets your mind focused on looking for solutions, systems, and strategies that you can control.

This is contrary to how most people start their day. Most people get up and start asking questions that are negative. They ask questions like "why don't I have any money?" or "who do I blame?"

The word "how" is written up on white board that I look at daily. It is there to remind me to ask myself a question that will keep my business growing. A famous question that I challenge my clients to ask of themselves is how do I get to the next level today? When you use a "how" question you will come up with a better answer, one that is positive, not negative.

By asking ourselves questions that start with the word how, we are curing the symptoms of the disease such as rationalization, procrastination, and fear.

Take for example the world of weight loss. This applies to entrepreneurs as many of us don't take care of ourselves the way we should. Many people say "I need to lose X". When my clients tell me that, I ask them two questions:

How much weight do you want to lose?

How much weight would you be happy losing?

I want you to know I have never found the two answers to be the same! Most people tell me, I need to lose 20lbs, but I would be happy with 10 lbs. When someone says that, what do you think the odds are of them losing 20lbs?

This mindset challenges entrepreneurial idiots in all aspects of their lives. This is the fear talking. Entrepreneurial idiots feel fear and then they let that fear control them. I want you to be different, I want you to acknowledge the fear, don't put up a safety net, don't procrastinate or rationalize.

I want you to move right through your fear by asking "how?". I want you to acknowledge that your success is the direct result of your work and it's not luck. I want you to get your mind focused daily on the right activities.

20 Minutes a Day Program

Getting your mind focused daily on the right activities won't happen by accident. One of the programs that I share with my clients is my 20 minutes a day program. It's a method that I developed and have used for over twenty years.

Putting this into action in your own life, simply means taking twenty minutes of quiet time daily. You can meditate, pray, or even sit in a dark room. Don't think about breaking it up into two sessions of ten minutes, it is essential to have twenty minutes of uninterrupted focused time.

What you will find when you do this is your mind will slow down. No longer will your mind be running at 9,000 RPM's. Your mind will slow and answers will become clear. The answers to even your toughest problems will be revealed when you can just slow your thoughts down daily. This exercise helps us to break through the fears we are feeling. You will be able to see clearly that fear is merely false evidence appearing real.

Your Assignment

Remember, I mentioned that change wasn't easy? Managing your fear won't come just by reading this book, it will only happen with action. This is a four part assignment. Complete these four parts and you will be on your way to curing entrepreneurial idiot disease.

Create a Link Page For Your Goals – Write down what you are linking to your goals. Even if you think you know it in your head already, get it down on paper. You might be surprised by the beliefs you are connecting to your goals. Save this paper and put it in front of you. When your links are negative you won't be able to attain your goals. You must change them to something positive.

Quiet Time – I want you to take twenty minutes daily to meditate, pray, and think. What change will be required to achieve your goals? What system can you put into action? What small step can you do today that will get you closer to your goals?

Stop Comparing Yourself to Others – The bottom line is that someone you know is making more money, is better looking, and better at many other things than you are. It's a waste of time and energy to compare yourself to other people.

Todd Bates Tips: Get downloads, cheat sheets, audio training, and more now by visiting: www.ToddBatesSystems.com /Resources

Become Aware of the Person Inside Your Head – There is a safe and conservative person who resides in your head. In contrast to this person is the real you. Be aware of these differences because usually the non-risky version of you is the one who is controlling your decisions. The more you become aware of who is controlling your decision making the quicker you will get to your deserved level of success.

Chapter 4 – Marketing for a 7 Figure Net Income & Preventing E.I.D from Crippling Response Rates

The constant in every single business I have ever owned is that it is powered by marketing. By focusing on marketing the business has a continued source of life.

When an entrepreneur tells me that "I don't market, I get 100% of my business from referrals" I know they have an issue in their business. Don't get me wrong, referrals are great in any business and many of my clients come from referrals. The real issue is when your business completely depends on referrals.

When you don't use marketing, you are dependent on your personality. Personality drives referrals. A business needs to have marketing at its core so that it can provide a consistent steady stream of new business regardless of economic conditions.

There are many misconceptions that entrepreneurs have in regards to marketing. I would like to reveal several of these so I can help you get to the next level.

The following are questions that I ask every single one of my clients, as well as audiences when I am conducting seminars. As you read through this chapter I would like you to answer these questions for yourself and your business. Having the written answers to these questions will give you a reference for change later.

2 Questions That Reveal Your Current Marketing Mindset

The first question is one that I have asked every client and every audience I have ever been in front of. The question can be phrased two ways. Regardless of how it is phrased, it is the same question.

What is your job?

What do you get paid to do?

This question seems obvious to many, however I would like you to look at the above questions for just a minute before you read below.

Over the years I have helped thousands of real estate agents get to the next level. When I ask them this question they answer, "To help clients buy and sell homes." 99% of audiences and clients answer the question this way prior to discovering their true purpose in their business. E.I.D entrepreneurs believe their job is to "help clients". I am not saying you shouldn't want to help your clients. However the goal of an entrepreneur is to find more business.

I can replace most entrepreneurs with someone who gets paid a fraction of what they are making to do their job. The hard part is always finding more business. I once had a chiropractor who said "You can't just have anyone do chiropractic work that is the hard part."

There are always new chiropractors graduating who may not have the capital to start their own business and need someone to work for. The hard part is still finding enough clients to be serviced. Without finding new clients, a business will go out of business. Remember earlier I mentioned that if you aren't growing you are dying.

Some of my clients even have a note above their computers that reminds them:

"My job is to find new business for my company and if I am not growing I am dying"

The second question that I need to ask you right now is going to put you on the path toward developing a marketing message that I will help you develop in this chapter. I would invite you to answer this question:

Why should people pick you?

Keep in mind this isn't for people who already know you and love you. We are talking about attracting new business. When someone doesn't know you, why should they decide to give you their business?

Any business has less than 10 seconds to make an impression on a total stranger. So the answer needs to get right to the point and clearly identify why someone should select your company.

E.I.D entrepreneurs answer the question, "Why should people pick you?" as follows:

- I am honest
- People like me
- I have experience
- I will work hard

- I won't lie or cheat them

Now let's be clear, is anyone out there looking for a company that lies, cheats, and won't work hard? No one is, so saying this is what customers expect.

I can't put on a website "I am honest" and have a prospect take action and fill out a form, request information, or purchase a product because they expect you to be honest.

There is a way to tell if your current marketing message will work. One of the tests that I perform for all of my clients is the white out test. This is how I can tell if they have a marketing message that will work or if it needs to be improved.

"Whiteout" Test Reveals Whose Marketing Will Generate Results

The whiteout test is one that you can do at home. I have my assistant do this for every new client. Every client has to send in their marketing pieces along with those of their competition. Everyone has competition so this is a good exercise to perform.

Once my assistant receives their marketing materials, she whites out the name of the company or web address so that I can't tell which marketing materials belong to my client and which ones belong to the competition.

When I can't tell the difference between my client's message and their competition, I know they need to change their marketing message. The message that they use must be powerful and instantly separate them from their competition.

95% of my clients fail this test right out of the gate. When you look and sound like everyone else there is no reason a prospect should contact you. The goal is to get more business. So we have to find a way to stand out from our competition.

There are four mistakes that entrepreneurs make when trying to craft their marketing message. I will reveal these to you so you may avoid these mistakes and start thinking about how you can change your message.

4 Biggest Mistakes Entrepreneurs Make In Marketing

Many entrepreneurs try marketing once and then stop because they felt it was "too expensive." Marketing is only expensive when it is done poorly. Avoiding these mistakes will put you on the path to generating results from your marketing.

#1 Mistake - Trying To Brand

The companies that can afford to brand are those that have names like Coca-Cola, IBM, and Toyota. Branding works when you have the budget to make it work.

Keep in mind; I am not saying that you shouldn't have a brand, identity, or even a logo. The mistake is when entrepreneurs spend their precious resources in marketing their brand to get their customers to identify with them.

Attracting new customers to you is about getting them to realize in 10 seconds or less how they benefit from doing business with your company. Entrepreneurs who desire to get out of survival mode will focus on having a powerful marketing message first and their brand will be second. When people don't know you they need to realize in seconds how they can benefit from your companies services or goods.

#2 Mistake – Unwilling to Take a Risk

Unless you have a product that is total garbage, I would suggest that you take a leap of faith and stand behind your product or service. I tell all of my clients "no one buys vanilla." In other words, ice cream stores don't make money from selling vanilla ice cream. They make money from the other flavors they offer.

How does this relate to your marketing message?

The safer you are, the more risky it is to your business. When you look, sound, and act like everyone else the risk to your business is tremendous. Customers will be unable to determine how you are different from your competition and this will lead to them not working with you.

#3 Mistake – Spending Too Much on Marketing

Just about every new client I have is initially scared to market their company because in the past they have "tried" marketing but it didn't work out very well. 100% of them haven't tried my marketing methods, which is why they seek me out.

Most entrepreneurs are spending too much on marketing when they are taking out ads, internet advertising, or any grassroots marketing approach.

One of the primary reasons I have always made money, regardless of economic conditions, is I am militant on marketing costs. I am always looking at how to increase a return on an ad and lower the cost at the same time.

The golden rule of marketing that I would suggest you adopt is not spending more than 7% of what a client is worth to you. For example, I have insurance agents as clients who make $500 on average per policy they sell. For them their 7% rule is $35. In other words they spend $35 and they get back $500.

Many entrepreneurs spend 50% of their income on marketing in the hopes that they will "grow" or make it back later. E.I.D entrepreneurs don't watch their costs and are in constant survival mode.

#4 Mistake – Relying On Your Personality

Many entrepreneurs rely 100% on their personality. They figure that they will make their business work and market "themselves."

When a new client or attendee says they are about to market their personality, I ask them the following:

"Have you ever started something and not finished?"

Relying on your personality will only lead toward poor results so I would encourage you not to make this mistake.

Marketing Message…an Entrepreneurs Key to Success

The silver bullet of entrepreneurial success is having a marketing message that you can bank your business on.

When you have a message that can resonate with any prospect that is even remotely interested in your product or service, and they feel compelled to contact you and not your competition, you have a message that will generate results.

A marketing message needs to have an extremely high perceived value to your potential customer, and at the same time inform them how it is risk free to take advantage of your product or service.

In a recent call with a client, he told me he had a product where he was offering a money back guarantee. This guarantee had been in practice for quite some time and as a result was not generating much of an increase in his sales. As I mentioned earlier, no one buys vanilla. All of his competitors offered the same 30 day money back guarantee.

The goal with a marketing message is to increase sales. We have to put ourselves in our customer's shoes and make ourselves a bit uncomfortable.

I asked my client how many of his customers ever returned his product. His return rate on his product was less than 2%. Bottom line he had a fantastic product that people loved. The challenge I put before him was how, with such a great product, he could make it even more risk free for new clients to try.

After our discussion we decided to change the guarantee to 120 days and 110% of the product. His guarantee was now 4 times as long as his competition and he was willing to pay them enough that they not only got their shipping covered they made a few dollars for their hassle as well.

This change increased his sales by 25% and his return rate only increased by 1%. Many entrepreneurs fear what would happen when they make it risk free to their clients. Regardless of the quality of your product there will always be someone who returns it. The key is to attract new clients who will end up falling in love with your product, become raving fans, and repeat customers.

Finding your marketing message is critical to your success. There are 8 categories of marketing messages that can separate you from your competition and bring you new valuable customers.

8 Marketing Messages That Will Change Your Business

When a new client asks me where they should start looking to develop a marketing message I ask them to review the 8 categories in the chart and get back to me on where they see themselves.

In order to make a marketing message work, you need to believe in it with your heart and soul. Having a marketing message based on one of theses 8 categories will keep you from being an E.I.D entrepreneur and put you on the path to success.

8 Categories of Marketing Messages

A marketing message must immediately attract the attention of the prospect. Combining one or more categories of marketing message will multiply the effectiveness of the message.
- Todd Bates

Before you continue on below I would ask you to take a moment to review the chart. Right now what I am going to ask you to do is to keep an open mind. Don't rule out any category yet until you have discovered in detail how each can be used to benefit your business.

Let's get into the 8 categories that will change your business.

Price of Your Products

Do you have a product or service that you can offer for less than your competition?

When an entrepreneur decides they want to compete on price, the first question I ask them is by how much they can beat their competition. For example, saying "I have the lowest prices" isn't impressive to a customer and won't draw attention to your business.

When you decide to have a marketing message based on the price of your products, you have to know by how much you can beat your competition. For example, if you can inform prospects that you beat your competition's prices by 10% that is extremely specific and powerful.

Another key success factor in competing on price is offering your prospects 3 choices. For example I have a real estate client who offers to sell a clients home for $795. His competition thinks he is absolutely crazy for offering to sell a clients property for $795.

The key to this message is that #1 he will absolutely sell someone's home for $795 and #2 he has two other choices that clients can select. When he meets with a client they get to select which plan they want to use to sell their home.

Competing on price works provided you have additional choices for the customer. When a customer is shopping on price they are often unaware of what additional services they could get should they spend slightly more money.

As for my real estate client, he offers 2 additional packages that provide additional services for an additional fee. The majority of clients select his other two packages because they desire the additional services he offers.

Quality of Your Product

Having a marketing message that will differentiate your physical products is a great way to separate yourself from your competition.

What is it that makes your product better than the competition?

I had a client that repaired watches. He told me his product was superior to every other watch store in town and I asked him, "Why?" What he was able to describe to me was a dissertation on the quality of the parts he used, the process he performed when assembling them, and how long they lasted after the repair was complete.

The detail that he was performing for his clients was over the top. The problem was that none of this was mentioned anywhere in his marketing.

People don't understand every business. Don't assume that every prospect has a clear idea of what it takes to perform the services your company delivers. When you can deliver your marketing message to anyone and they clearly see the benefits you are providing them you are on your way to a successful marketing message.

This category, quality of product, works provided you inform your prospects of the details on how your product or service is different.

Extra Services

Many of my clients provide so much service to their clients it is almost disgusting. Are you providing services for free that your competition is charging for?

This can be a great way to differentiate yourself from your competition especially when your competition can offer a lower price 100% of the time. Thinking outside the box and offering additional services that cost you very little yet have a high perceived value can help you get a higher price for your product.

One of my clients sells TV's. For just a minute I would like you to think about his competition. He is competing on some level against Wal-mart, Target, and BestBuy. There is absolutely no way that he can compete on price. When I asked him how he was different he informed me that he provided two additional services to all of his clients.

He delivered all of his TV's free and he provided them with a free extended warranty. These are two very important extra services that he was providing to clients, yet was not using in his marketing. The warranty alone was worth hundreds of dollars and none of the big box stores offered a free warranty. A customer purchasing through him was getting hundreds of dollars in value and most of all peace of mind with the warranty.

Delivery was another extremely valuable extra service he was providing to his clients. As TV's have become larger, many home owners don't own vehicles that can fit the TV in the protective box it comes in. His delivery was saving home owners from having to borrow a friend's vehicle or pay a delivery charge.

Extra services don't have to cost you money, but they just must have a highly perceived value to your customer.

Another client of mine in the Denver area owns a Mexican restaurant. The restaurant business is a very competitive business so finding a way to differentiate your business is critical.

Since I had recently been to his restaurant I asked him if he just gave me the free chips and salsa or if they were provided free to all his guests. They were absolutely fantastic chips and salsa and my family was raving about them days later. He informed me that he had always offered free chips and salsa to all of his guests.

His competition, other Mexican restaurants in the Denver area, all charged for chips, salsa, or both. He had a fantastic extra that he was offering to his clients that he was not taking advantage of. I developed a marketing message for him that took advantage of the chips and salsa offer that he was providing to his diners.

When looking at developing a marketing message around extras, write down in detail what you provide for your clients. Then, look at your list compared to your competition. Even the smallest items may be extremely valuable to your prospects.

Communication

There are many businesses that have amazing communication with their clients. Many of my clients communicate on a near daily basis with their clients through e-mail, phone, and fax. They provide this high level of communication to provide an outstanding level of customer service to their clients which in turn generates more business for them.

Entrepreneurs who provide high touch services need to clearly demonstrate to their future prospects this benefit in their marketing message.

A client of mine is an attorney who performs wills and trusts. In his area of business the majority of attorneys charged $3,000 per client. I asked my client what level of communication he provided to his clients.

He informed me that when they asked a question he had a very detailed answer for them. He presented me with a detailed packet of information that had hundreds of detailed answers. I asked him if his competition had such packets. Most of his competition would just verbally inform the clients of the answers to their questions.

What we discussed doing was turning his packet of information into a set of answers that the clients received before they had the question. The goal is to turn a feature of your business, product, or service into a benefit to the client.

We were able to turn his packet of information into a powerful marketing message because we stressed how it was a benefit to the client. He was able to use this to separate himself from his competition and increase the amount he charged per client. The average value of his client went up to nearly $5,000 per client. Clients were willing to pay more for the service.

Communication is critical in businesses, and in the majority of cases you can increase the price you charge for your product or service as a result of your level of communication.

Testimonials

The best sales force a company can have is the past clients who have used the product or service. One of the reasons testimonials are great is that they do the selling for you. When a prospect can see that others who are in similar situations have tried your product or service, and it has worked out well, they are more likely to take action.

Trail blazers, those who are first to try a product, are few and far between, so testimonials provide a great way to let others know the path is safe for them to travel.

At seminars I routinely ask the audience "Do your clients love you?"

The answers is a general nodding of heads and "yes Todd my clients love me." Entrepreneurs provide great customer service in general so this is to be expected.

My next question is always the following and I would invite you to answer it as well:

"How many testimonials do you have?"

Surprisingly, the answer is always very low. At one seminar, a mortgage lender informed me that he had 20 testimonials. I asked him how many clients he had helped over the course of doing business and the number was in the thousands.

Most entrepreneurs are not taking advantage of the power of testimonials for their business. To make testimonials effective, they need to reach our intended audience in the correct format and be truthful.

Testimonials can be in audio, video, or written form. Let's take a look at how each of these should be used in order to be most effective.

- **Audio testimonials**. Getting your client to record their voice talking about your product is extremely powerful. There are plenty of services that you can use to have your client easily record a testimonial. I reference some of these services in the resources chapter at the end of this book, and even more on the website for this book. When recording audio testimonials, have your clients be themselves. They don't need to be over the top with an endorsement, they just need to discuss how they came about finding you, their situation, and what they thought of the experience. Sometimes they may even share a partial negative opinion of your company, product, or service and how you fixed the issue. This only makes the testimonial more real and effective.
- **Video testimonials**. Video is one of my favorite mediums and I believe it will continue to be more effective as time goes on. Many people don't want to record video because of how they feel they will look, sound and act. However getting video is extremely beneficial to your business. Future clients can watch

videos on your website, Facebook Fan Page, or even on a DVD.

- **Written testimonials**. Over the years written testimonials have been abused. Some of them have been faked which has lowered their effectiveness. However, there is a way to avoid this by following a few simple written testimonial rules. When working with written testimonials, having the client put it on their company letterhead will increase the power of the endorsement. A testimonial with your client's signature on it or even in their own hand writing is also effective. Many of my clients say that their past clients are even willing to have their real phone numbers used in testimonials. When they offer this, take them up on it. The majority of prospects will not call them. When a prospect does call one of your past clients it is extremely effective.

When using testimonials as a marketing message, the trick becomes getting them. The easiest time to get a testimonial is when you are working with the client. For my clients that work face to face with their customers, I recommend always keeping a video camera handy or using their cell phones to record the audio. Having expensive equipment isn't necessary anymore. Affordable devices are easily available to record both video and audio.

For my clients that deal exclusively on the Internet, it is important to make getting testimonials a system. When offering extras to your clients, getting testimonials can be as simple as offering an extra that every client really wants.

I have a client who sells exclusively on the Internet. He sells physical products and his best clients buy something from him every 3 months. In exchange for a testimonial, he offers them free expedited shipping on their next order. The testimonials generate far more sales than the small amount of money it costs for the expedited shipping.

You can never have too many testimonials. The important part is to craft a message around the happy clients that are willing to share their experience with others.

Statistics

Statistics is one of my favorite marketing message categories. It is a powerful category because every business is going to be able to find at least one if not two or three statistics that separates them from their competition. Crafting a marketing message around a killer statistic is powerful and can greatly increase the leads and sales for a business.

Analytical individuals love statistics because it gives them specifics they can focus on. When looking for a statistic, the goal is to find something that is extremely important to the customer and put it in a clear and concise message that immediately draws their attention.

I work with a number of insurance agents from a variety of companies. I asked one of my clients what was important to her clientele. In her market, everyone needed desperately to save money. People love saving money.

Saving money is great, however putting "I will save you money" is vague and not a statistic that I can use effectively to help an insurance agent increase their business. I asked her to find out for me how much money on average she was able to save her clients in comparison to her competition. She owned a franchise and her parent company was able to provide the information. Even my independent insurance agent clients are able to get this kind of information easily.

For her market, she was saving clients on average 11.2% more than her competition. I crafted multiple marketing messages for her around the percentage, dollar amount, and even how long she spent with a client.

We related all of her statistics to specific points that the customer cares about. From her past interactions with her customers she was able to provide me with her prospects biggest frustration points with the insurance industry. Addressing a customer's frustration in a marketing message is extremely effective to generate more sales.

Prospects don't act out of comfort, they act out of pain. Relating a specific statistic, that will relieve the pain in their situation, is a great way to increase your number of leads. More leads equal more sales.

The bottom line on statistics is to look for what you do best in comparison to your competition or the industry average. Spending just a few minutes to find what I call a "Killer Statistic" will go a long way to increasing your sales.

Service Category

Across the country I have clients who are salesmen who work for larger companies. Their entire job is to drum up sales on a daily basis. Their companies provide them with "support" and "marketing materials" but no leads.

All of my clients in this situation are looking for an edge on their competition. This category works well when you have help and support in your business.

Many of my clients have entire support teams dedicated to supporting their product after the sale. I have a number of clients who sell home warranties. Their clients are home owners and real estate agents. They sell the home warranty, yet their parent company handles all of the service calls and any other work after the sale of the policy.

I asked one of my clients "How many people help you behind the scenes?"

When she thought about the support staff, toll free help line, and service contractors who performed the work, the minimum number of people who supported her sales was 437.

Clients who chose to purchase a policy through her were not just getting her; they were getting 437 people to help them in case an incident arose. Not only was this a larger number, this was actually twice as many support staff as her competition offered.

Prospects and clients love getting more than they paid for. When someone finds out they are getting more, they feel like they are getting a deal (because they are) and they buy more.

This marketing message works great when you have help behind the scenes. Often we don't realize we have help behind the scenes, so for my entrepreneurs who are on their own, I always ask them "do you have any business partners?"

Most of us don't do 100% of the work for each and every client. When crafting a marketing message around the service category, taking credit for all of your support staff will increase the response you get from this type of message.

Guarantees

The guarantee category is the most powerful category available to an entrepreneur. The primary reason that guarantees work so well is that prospects love them. When you are developing a marketing message with a guarantee, I want you to think of how you can eliminate risk for the prospect.

When a prospect sees that it is risk free to try your product or service, they will take action. Having a guarantee requires some fear management. E.I.D entrepreneurs are often unwilling to guarantee their product or service, or their guarantee is so weak it is the same as not having a guaranteed message at all.

As an example, having a "30 Day Money Back Guarantee" worked great 15 years ago, but now that is expected by the prospect. A guarantee needs to separate yourself from your competition. It needs to pull the prospect in and get them to take action.

The farther out that you are willing to go on a guarantee, the more money you are going to make. I don't want to repeat myself, but for just a moment I would like you to think about your financial goal. Now that you have that dollar amount in your head, I would like to ask you the same question I ask my clients and attendees of my seminars:

What could you guarantee if I made you guarantee something?

When looking to craft a message around a guarantee, I like to remind my clients of two items:

1. People are, for the most part, honest and really want a product or service to work
2. Regardless of whether you provide a guarantee or not there will always be someone who is going to try and rip you off

Creating a guarantee message is about attracting more clients to your door so you can make more money.

I had a client who was offering the standard "30 Day Money Back Guarantee." All of his competitors were also offering this same guarantee. His guarantee was not increasing his business in the least.

When I asked him how many people ever returned his product he said that 5% of purchases ended up returned. 5% is a very low return rate. If he was able to generate more sales, he was ok even if a few more people returned his product.

Throughout our discussion I asked how confident he was in his product. He said his customers loved the product and continued to send him referrals after they purchased the product. I crafted a message for him that provided customers with a 200% guarantee. Prospects not only had no risk in buying the product, they were going to be paid if they didn't like the product.

The more risk free you can make it for your prospects the more sales you will make. The message increased his sales by 27%. His returns increased from 5% to 8% but the profits more than made up for the difference.

He was willing to go out on a limb to provide prospects with a guarantee on his product. An E.I.D entrepreneur would never go out on a limb because they would allow their fear to take over. He was able to control his fear to run the guarantee and he was rewarded with the increase in sales.

Guarantees are only powerful if they clearly explain to the prospect how it is a risk free purchase. The safer they feel about trying out your product or service, the more likely they are to take action with your business.

For the guarantee category I would like you to think of the following:

- How safe can I make my prospects feel?
- What can I guarantee my prospects?
- How far am I willing to go?

Your Assignment
Developing you marketing message may be the most important item you ever do for your business. Once you have a marketing message for your business you can begin to build a long term marketing foundation.

To get the most out of this process I would invite you to do the following steps undisturbed without distraction. That means you must find a place where the TV is turned off, the dog isn't barking, and the neighbor kids drum set can't be heard.

In the first part of the process I would ask you to pick a category for your marketing message. Select one category that you are willing to put your time, effort, and money in. You must feel passionate about the category so the rest of the process will flow through to the final creation.

After you have selected a category I want you to develop a message around the category you select. Put yourself in your customer's shoes and put down what you would want to see if you didn't know your company and was considering making a purchase.

Upon completion of your message creation the next step is to make it the first item that every customer sees about your company.

Spread your marketing message through everything your company does via mail, the Internet, fax, and e-mail.

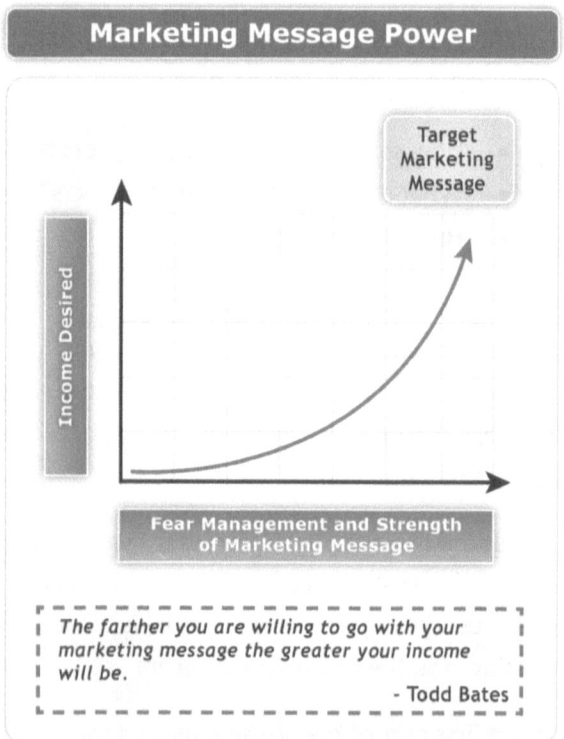

The power of your marketing message will dictate your income level. In the chart I have outlined how the power of a marketing message has an exponential return on your income.

In other words the farther out you are willing to go with your marketing message, and the more prospects see your message, the more your sales will increase. For additional information, resources, and training guides on developing your own marketing message please visit www.ToddBatesSystems.com/Resources.

Chapter 5 – Stop Looking Like a Salesman & Start Making More Money Now

Sales and Conversion Techniques That Prevent E.I.D

Entrepreneurial idiots sometimes forget there are two sides to business. As you discovered in the marketing chapter, it is imperative to define your business with a marketing message. Mastering that part of the business will make your phone ring, get your website blazing, and have your email inbox full of eager contacts. If that was all there was to it, there would be many more successful entrepreneurs, but that is just one side of the business.

Getting free from entrepreneurial idiot disease and becoming a smart entrepreneur means embracing the sales conversion side of the business. I am not talking about having the gift of gab or being someone who is naturally good with people. Quite honestly, most entrepreneurs who say they are great with people talk too much, and as a result their conversion rate drops! The more you talk to your prospects the more you look like a salesman, and salesmen are broke. I am going to challenge you to be different, and the more you change the greater your success.

Before I share with you the six categories of sales and conversion, I invite you to discover the characteristics that most entrepreneurial idiots suffer from.

How Entrepreneurial Idiots Stay Trapped With Poor Conversion Rates

I have seen thousands of entrepreneurs struggle with the same challenges. They have leads, more than they need to meet their current sales goals, yet they struggle to reach their quotas.

Over time I have found that the challenges entrepreneurs face with conversion fall into three main categories regardless of their industry. Regardless of where your conversion issues are currently occurring you will discover they fall into one of the following three categories.

Not Having A Clear Marketing Message

By now you have probably developed your marketing message. Most entrepreneurial idiots simply don't have one. They rely on their personality to get people to contact them and that leaves them in survival mode. Stop relying on your personality, stop looking and sounding like everyone else and be different!

When you can't be differentiated from others in your industry, you won't be able to have a high conversion rate. The reason standing out with your marketing message is so vital is not just because it makes your phone ring, it's because you get to use it in your conversations.

They Try to Sell Over the Phone

I know I am encouraging you to put your marketing plan into action, but that doesn't mean selling on the phone. Entrepreneurial idiots try and "sell" everyone who calls them something. They figure "any sale is better than no sale". This attitude keeps your business in survival mode.

When people express interest in your product or service, your job is not to sell them over the phone. Your job is merely to pique their interest enough to take the next step in your sales cycle. I don't want you sounding like a cheesy used car salesman with lines like "can I make you color blind?" trying to get the sale at that moment.

Let me be direct with you, as I am in the sales and marketing industry myself. No one likes a salesperson! Bottom line, people don't like to be sold, and they don't like salespeople. I want you to understand the difference between sounding like a slick car salesman and using a consulting approach.

A cheesy car salesman does whatever he can to cram you into the sale. He spouts off miles per gallon numbers, endless options, and tries to tell you things that are not important to your decision without even asking you. This approach often gives people the feeling of being under a heat lamp. When you feel brave, you head immediately off the lot as the salesman tries to chase after you.

The consultative approach is an approach like the one your Doctor uses. As a consultant to your prospects you should ask questions. After they answer your initial questions, you can dig deeper with even more questions. Each question gives you more insight into their goals and helps the consumer realize what is important to them. You artfully guide them to the only logical decision, which is to invest in what you are offering.

Who would you prefer to buy from, the car salesman or the consultant? Your approach might not be as extreme as the car salesman, but I can tell you that those who suffer from E.I.D. aren't asking the right questions.

Worrying Too Much About "Closing"

Too many movies have made closing seem more important than it really is. Phrases like "always be closing" are shouted out among sales offices across the country. This mindset will keep you broke! Here is the reality: Closing Never Works! People are too smart to be "closed" on. Even if you can convince a few weak minded people to buy your product, they will surely return it after they get off the phone with you.

Stop worrying about the right moment to close. There is no need to memorize 132 different closing statements. When you think of closing, I want you to consider that you are trying to "trick" someone into making a purchase. You don't really want to trick people do you? Of course not, so stop closing.

Now on the extreme end, I don't want you being so helpful that you don't convert. Instead of closing, I invite you to consider that you are looking for a match. In every conversation you are looking to find out if your prospect has a need that matches up with the product or service you are offering. You can only find this match when you ask questions.

There are some people who approach me at my seminars when I share not to close and tell me, "but Todd, I am like the greatest sales person. I can sell ice to Eskimos." I can tell you that these people are broke. People don't like salespeople, it just doesn't work. Besides, it's easy to sell Eskimos ice in the summer, because they need it! You can't talk people into buying something they don't want or need.

I need you to really get in your head how important it is to stop worrying about closing. I had a client of mine call me about the leads he was getting from his website. He told me the leads were just pouring in as a result of the marketing plan I had him put into action. He didn't call to thank me. He called to tell me that MOST of the leads were not turning into sales! I asked him what his conversion rate was, and he told me 10%.

I shared with him that his number was about right. Marketing is about getting people to raise their hand and express interest. You won't close or convert each lead into a sale. In fact I have what I call the 85% rule. The 85% rule is quite simple. 85% of leads are just a total waste of time and energy. The more you realize that a huge portion of any lead source is a waste of time, the easier it becomes to ask the right questions to get to that top 15%.

Get Out Of Being an Entrepreneurial Idiot and Into Being a Smart Entrepreneur

Transforming yourself from being an entrepreneurial idiot into a smart entrepreneur takes change. It won't happen overnight. It will be challenging, but it will get you out of survival mode. I would invite you to consider that this transformation will take shape quickly by avoiding key negative behaviors.

You will be on the road to being a smart entrepreneur when you don't look and act like a salesperson. You will start making more sales when you don't try and convince your prospect. You will start enjoying your business more when you don't try to persuade people. Should you not avoid these bad habits, you will look like a salesperson, and salespeople make $75,000 a year.

Smart entrepreneurs surpass their income goals because they focus on six different categories of sales and conversion that they look to perfect and master. A smart entrepreneur will look to these processes and understand that it really is a numbers game.

Categories of Sales and Conversion that Will Increase Your Sales

The six categories of sales and conversion that I will share with you are what smart entrepreneurs work to master. They understand that you can't tackle every conversion category at the same time. Being a smart entrepreneur means knowing that you don't want to be like everyone else. You want to

6 Categories of Sales Conversion

Marketing Message

Interest Piquing Questions

Voice Mail

Sales & Appointments

Over the phone

Call Back

Face to Face

Mastering one conversion category will give you a 6 figure net income. Mastering 4 out of 6 categories will net you 7 figures.

- Todd Bates

be different, because when you are different you will achieve mastery and you will have the business of your dreams.

The entrepreneurial idiot tries to tackle all of the categories of conversion at once and ends up mastering none of them. As you go through each category, challenge yourself to identify with one that you will attack by the end of the chapter. Being able to identify the category that is your biggest challenge will help you move farther along the road to being a smart entrepreneur.

The chart at the beginning of this chapter outlines the categories that I will be covering. At this moment what I am going to ask you to do is to keep your options open.

Understanding Your Marketing Message

Your marketing message, when used on your website, postcards, and direct mail, will generate leads. It will generate phone calls, emails, and maybe even faxes. More important than simply sticking your marketing message everywhere is using it in your conversations.

Despite our love for technology, ranging from simple websites to Twitter, the big money is still being made in conversations. It's honestly tough in today's world to get anything done without using the phone. Sure you can sell cheap CD's and books online without talking to people, but the major sales numbers are still driven by your skill on the phone. The greater your skill on the phone, the better your business will become. When you can integrate your marketing message throughout your phone conversations, prospects will transform themselves into customers. I need you to stop being a free information service and start being a marketing professional.

Here is what I mean by being a marketing professional on the phone. I want you to ask your prospect questions that specifically relate to your message. You can ask questions for any type of message that you are offering. For example, if you were using the guarantee marketing message, you could ask your prospect, "do you know of anyone else that will offer this type of guarantee?" This is a good way to remind them of how you are different, and how you don't sound like everyone else.

Many of my clients are in the real estate field. The real estate agents that struggle look and sound like everyone else. Real estate agents that work with me typically use a guarantee marketing message such as, "I will sell your home in 39 days or less, or I will sell it for Free...Guaranteed." That message doesn't sound like anyone else! Now, when the agent is on the phone, they can ask the prospect, "Will anyone else that you are interviewing guarantee to sell your home in 39 days or less?"

This way, you get the benefit of reminding your prospect of your marketing message. Notice that you are asking questions about your marketing message, not making statements. You want to avoid statements such as, "remember, I guarantee to sell your home in "X days". No one likes to be told what to do especially a prospect considering your product or service. Simply ask questions that will remind your prospect of how different your products and services are, compared to the competition.

Integrating your message into your conversations isn't limited to just the category of guarantees. Should you be using the testimonial category, you could ask your prospect a powerful, interest piquing question like, "how many testimonials would you like to see in order to give me a shot?" This reminds them of the 100, or 200+ testimonials that you have on your website.

The rules don't change for the service and pricing categories of marketing messages. Ask questions that will remind your prospects of your message. If you are using a service message, you could ask them, "would you rather have 1 person working on your account or 5?" When you are in an industry that is price sensitive, and you are using the pricing category message, you can pique your prospects interest by asking them, "Do you know anyone else who will sell "X" for as low as "Y"?

No matter what your marketing message, you have to insert it into your conversations. You really only "have to" put your marketing message into conversations when you want conversion. Develop questions around your message and put them next to your phone. Make sure to use them on every phone call.

Over the Phone Conversion

Phone conversion is one of the tougher areas of mastery. It is tough for many entrepreneurial idiots because they have so many bad habits to break. Remember, entrepreneurial idiots try to sell on the phone, which is a total disaster!

You can break the mold, and start having phenomenal success on the phone, when you focus on three ways to get your prospects attention. In some conversations you may enlist all three of these techniques.

Get Their Attention in the First Sentence

Most people have short attention spans. People on the internet and on the phone are barely paying attention, which makes it imperative to grab their attention immediately. I don't want you wasting time on rapport building, or asking if they have time to talk with you. I want you snapping them to attention in the first ten seconds of a conversation.

To get their attention almost immediately, I want you to think of an outrageous question. A question so over the top it would make your competition squirm. It must be so bold that someone would nearly think you are crazy just for asking. For example, if you were in the world of copier sales, like many of my clients, you could ask a question like, would you like to discover how to cut your copying costs by 37%?

What businesses wouldn't want to cut their copying costs by 37%? Once that question is out there, you will have your prospects undivided attention. No longer will they be playing solitaire while they are talking to you. They will be totally focused on what you are sharing with them. Now that you have their attention, you have the opportunity to launch an arsenal of questions.

Match Script

The match script is one of my favorites because it reduces the anxiety of your prospect and puts you immediately in the driver seat. The reality is that people put up walls in every conversation. We are naturally conditioned to want to reject what someone has to offer until we can see a massive benefit. With the match script as part of your conversion strategy, you will be able to get the prospect to lower their barriers, and be open to what you have to say, for the remainder of the conversation.

At the beginning of the conversation, I would invite you to state the following "I am not trying to sell you [your product], I am just trying to find out if there is a match between what you are looking for and what I have to offer."

I typically emphasize the word "sell" in order for the prospect to understand that I am not like everyone else. This puts the prospect in a mode where they are now trying to determine HOW they can fit your product into their business

Identify Your Prospects Biggest Fear
This one takes skill. You won't just be identifying your prospect's fear; you will be using it against them! It takes a bit of practice to make sure it doesn't come across like you are attacking them. However, master this one and prospects will be eager to work with you.

Let's take an example from the field of real estate. In real estate, buyers have a great deal of fear and apprehension about the process. Instead of empathizing with their fears, dig deep and expose them! You could ask them an arsenal of questions such as; Are you afraid of overpaying? Are you concerned that you might get sued after the transaction closes? Do you know what should be done if you encounter major problems with the home during an inspection?

By asking questions that attack their fears you have no longer allowed them to hide behind common objections. You have brought their deepest darkest fears into the light, and they will be forced to face them! With their fears exposed, they will look to someone who can help them solve these problems, and thankfully you are already on the phone.

Face to Face Conversion
Many people under estimate the power of face to face conversion. Entrepreneurial idiots figure by the time they have the face to face meeting, the prospect is as good as "sold." That is where the problems begin. Getting meetings is great, but making sales gives you a net income.

Mastering face to face conversion is absolutely critical. How critical? 93% of sales and conversion result from non-verbal communication. That means, 93% of your success will be dictated not by what you say, but how you say it. It is absolutely imperative that your focus be on the prospect. That might sound obvious, but what I have found when working with my coaching clients is that in most face to face meetings their focus is on their presentation, their product, or their PowerPoint. Not on the prospect, where it should be.

Focusing on your prospect in face to face meetings is what will give you conversion rates over 90%. Your focus starts from the first few moments that you meet them. I want you to greet them with a strong handshake, use their first name, and even be aware of how they are sitting. Getting your prospect to take action by the end of the meeting means taking the time to mirror your prospect.

Here is what I mean. I need you to commit yourself to the prospect with all of your energy. Make sure you have high energy when you are face to face. No one likes to work with someone who is vague, general, and not exciting. When it comes to this type of conversion, many of my clients need some work because they have been relying on talking. Remember, what you say is only 7% of the game, and that is what most people are relying on to get the sale.

If you focus your energy into acting like your prospect, sounding more like your prospect, and bringing your excitement level up, they will gravitate to you. If you want to get your conversion rate up, you must take the time to focus on non-verbal communication, which is 93% of what makes the sale.

Call Back Sales and Conversion
This area of conversion is focused on how you will be converting people when you call them back from their initial request.

E.I.D – Entrepreneurial Idiot Disease

www.ToddBatesBook.com/Resources

When you are generating leads people will give you their contact information, but you still need to get a hold of them to make the sale. Using the correct methods and scripts when calling people back can easily increase your sales volume by 40%. When most entrepreneurial idiots call people back they are too helpful, which simply ruins your conversion rate.

The key to mastering conversion comes down to four different scripts. Only put these scripts into action when you want to start making more sales from the leads you are generating.

Missing Information Script
I tell my clients that the purpose of their brochure, magazine ads, letters, websites, etc is to pique someone's interest. You don't want to give all of the information or your marketing won't generate any results. When you leave out a part of the information that is essential to your prospect, you give them a reason to reach out to you.

Let's look at the field of real estate. In real estate, when people are looking for homes, the price is the number one item that they want to know. If you put the prices of homes on your website and ads, potential clients have no reason to contact you. The crucial part is getting people to call! When you are calling leads back from your ads, you know they are going to ask for price, but that is merely the start of the conversation (hint: don't give them the price at the beginning of your conversation.) When calling them back you can simply state, "I see you called, was there a specific piece of information you were looking for?" After this, you can launch into an arsenal of 132 different questions to get the appointment.

Many of my entrepreneurial idiots simply give away all of the information. They reveal in their ads all the information someone would need. They share price, options, features, etc, and quite frankly I am surprised some of their ads get any calls. Leave information missing and you will start getting more calls that lead to more conversion and more sales.

Motivation Script

By using the motivation script, you will be able to quickly determine where someone is in the buying cycle. Most of my clients don't want someone who is early in the "research" phase; they want someone who can take action today. Finding prospects that are willing to take action doesn't mean extensive qualifying scripts; it comes down to determining their level of motivation.

Take another example from the field of real estate. In real estate, finding out if a prospect has bought or sold a home before is imperative to determining your next set of questions. In order to cut to the chase and find their motivation, my real estate clients ask, I'm just calling you back to see if this is your first time buying or selling a home?"

By asking a question that reveals to you what their past experience is, you will be able to focus in on their fears right away.

Specific Program Script

In almost every industry there are programs that are offered to incentivize customers to take action. Every industry from auto manufacturers to real estate has special programs that can push that hesitant prospect into taking action.

Before I share with you the specific program script, I want to be very clear. Don't reveal all of the information on the program! Most people who suffer from entrepreneurial idiot disease are so helpful when they return the prospects call, that the prospect has no reason to meet with them. They eliminate their chances of getting the sale because they reveal too much.

A recent program that affected the auto industry, and many of my clients, was the cash for clunkers program. This program gave consumers the opportunity to bring in their old cars and get a rebate they could use towards the purchase or lease of a new vehicle.

I shared with my clients in the auto industry that their sales professionals should not reveal all of the information on the program. I helped them develop scripts to get customers to come to their car lots so they could make more sales. Instead of sharing everything about a program to a customer on the phone, I had them ask questions like, "were you going to be using the cash for clunkers program for this purchase? Or, did you want do determine if your current vehicle qualified for the cash for clunkers program?" This brought people onto their car lots in waves to see if their cars qualified, because they didn't know about all of the details of this specific program.

The bottom line is that nearly every industry has specific incentive programs available. The smart entrepreneur uses these programs to convert prospects into customers.

Make them an Offer Script
Having multiple ways to connect with a customer is a sure fire way to increase your sales. As you generate leads, you may not have all of the customer's information that you want (like

address, email, etc). To get additional contact information from your prospects, I would encourage you to make them an offer.

For example, when you are calling a prospect back, you could simply say, "I was just calling you back to get your email and give you "X". It doesn't matter what you give them, you have now deepened the relationship, added value, and gotten more information from them. In the case of email, you can never have enough email addresses in your marketing database.

The important point with call back conversion is it is nearly impossible to get someone on the phone on the first call! Having the four call back conversion scripts is an essential part of your sales arsenal and will keep you from being a struggling entrepreneurial idiot.

Using Interest Piquing Questions

Most sales people don't use interest piquing questions. In fact most sales people make too many statements, and end up going into "sales mode" which only results in rejection. People who remain plagued with entrepreneurial idiot disease can't grab their prospects attention. They can't get their prospects to see how they are different.

Separating yourself from your competition requires piquing people's interest. Interest piquing questions make it obvious for a prospect to want to find out more information. I would challenge you to develop questions that would make it crazy for someone NOT to want more information from you. Consider the following three questions:

Would you like to find out how to save $300 on your next purchase of "X"?

Would you like to discover how to get this product or service delivered in the next 22 days?

Would you like to find out the 1 thing you absolutely have to do BEFORE you buy this product or service that will save you time and money?

Looking at those questions, if you were a motivated prospect, wouldn't you want to find out the answers? Remember, we are looking for that top 15% of prospects who want to do business with us. When people are really interested in taking action, they would be crazy not to find out how they could save time and money.

I have found interest piquing questions to be one of the most essential tools for the smart entrepreneur. To help cure your entrepreneurial idiot disease I created an entire website and product just around interest piquing questions. It's a collection of questions that anyone can use immediately in their business. You can find out even more about interest piquing questions by visiting www.QuestionsThatSell.com.

Voicemail Conversion

Voicemail conversion is a combination of the other methods. The worst thing you can do is leave messages like everyone else. Most entrepreneurial idiots leave messages like, "I was just calling to follow up on your request, please call me at 555-555-5555."

You might be thinking that you just shouldn't leave voicemails; wrong! It is a waste of time to leave average voicemails. Leaving the right voicemails will have prospects chasing you down for your expertise. To get prospects watering at the mouth to speak with you one must incorporate different conversion methods in your messages.

Todd Bates Tip: Get sample plans that my clients use to put their categories into action:
www.ToddBatesSystems.com /Resources

You should leave messages that reveal your marketing message, or ask interest piquing questions. Just envision listening to your voicemail from someone who followed up with you and said, "I was following up from your request. I invite you to call back when you want to find out how to save $300 on your next purchase of "X", you can reach me at 555-555-5555." That is a voicemail that piques interest! Just make it obvious in your messages what you would like the prospect to call back about and your phone will be ringing non-stop.

Your Assignment

Curing yourself from entrepreneurial idiot's disease is about discovering new methods which make it easy to improve your sales conversion. Instead of tackling all six of the categories of conversion at once, I want you to pick just one.

After you pick your category, I want you to create a new plan, a new approach, and a new way of inserting that category into your business. It could be as simple as writing out interest piquing questions and putting them next to your phone for use in your conversations. My point is to make your plan and approach simple in order to make is easy for you to stick with.

Now, with your plan in place, practice this new approach for 2-3 weeks. It doesn't matter which one you tackle first, just put it into action for a few weeks. Don't stray, don't start another project, just put the one category into your business.

Once you have gotten comfortable with your one category, then and only then you can pick another category. Repeat the cycle until you have gone through all six. Remember, entrepreneurial idiots never get to the next level because they try to do too much at once. Smart entrepreneurs look at the six categories, tackle one at a time, improve it, and tweak it, master it, and then they move on.

Start accomplishing more today by putting your one category into action.

Chapter 6 – Creating More Time in Your Business...Guaranteed

Every entrepreneur has said at least once "if I only had more time." Time management is one of the biggest issues that face entrepreneurs. The faster an entrepreneur can discover how they can get more time out of their day, the more money they will make and the more time off they will have.

99% of entrepreneurs are terrible at time management because it is a fundamental personality flaw. All of us in the entrepreneurial world have ideas, projects, and a vision for our companies that constantly pull us in all directions.

The best that an entrepreneur can really hope for in regards to time management is improving on their current situation. Your time management skills will never be perfect because mastering time management and being an entrepreneur just don't match up.

The good news about all of this is that after having worked with entrepreneurs over the last 20 years, and being one myself, I have discovered several tasks that everyone can put into place to generate results.

Right now the only time management task that I am going to ask you to master is to finish this chapter. Sometimes as an entrepreneur we get distracted, so for now turn the phone off, find a quiet place, and discover how you can accomplish the goal of squeezing more time out of your day.

www.ToddBatesBook.com/Resources

E.I.D. Time Management Symptoms That Prevent Entrepreneurs from Success

A recent client of mine suggested that they didn't have a time management problem. We were speaking about how they never seemed to reach their income goals yet they always were "busy."

This leads to me to look into what at an entrepreneur does with their day and how it can be changed. Entrepreneurs with time management issues, nearly all entrepreneurs, face the following symptoms that prevent them from getting the most out of their day.

The Telephone

At a seminar, on a break, an attendee came up to me and said "Todd I go through over 5,000 cell phone minutes a month." He said this with a sense of pride before his phone rang yet again and he answered it with his blue tooth headset.

I call these people the "Crackberry" crowd. They are constantly available to their clients, their employees, and everyone else in their life. There isn't a single moment of the day, including the five minutes they visit the bathroom, that they don't answer the phone.

Cell phones have only made this problem worse for entrepreneurs as they can now be constantly connected to their businesses. When the minutes on your cell phone bill are in the 1,000's the telephone is probably one of the symptoms of time management that you are facing.

Do Everything Themselves

On almost every coaching call with every client I have I hear the following "But Todd you don't understand, no one can do it better than I can." To be honest, early on in my career, I struggled with this symptom.

I was the guy who used to do everything myself. I, just like my clients now, never had time to get things done because I was the one doing everything.

Recently I had a call with a client who is a mortgage broker. Over the years many of my clients have been in the real estate industry. This mortgage broker had a successful business however he never seemed to have time. This seemed strange to me at first because I knew that he had a receptionist, a loan processor, and an assistant. He had a staff so he should actually have had more time on his hands and have been making more money.

After asking several questions I discovered that while my client had help, he was still effectively doing everything himself. His approval was needed for almost every facet of his business. His assistant couldn't even send a simple fax without him reviewing it and initializing it to be sent.

He was terrible at delegation and was holding his business back. E.I.D entrepreneurs who are having time management issues often have staff, yet they fail to delegate.

Do you have staff now, whether full time, part time, or outsourced?

For now I would just like you to take note if you have staff and we will discuss how smart entrepreneurs use their staff.

Working ALL the Time

99% of entrepreneurs aren't lazy. They are some of the hardest working people in America. Working all the time can take its toll and many entrepreneurs don't even realize they are doing it.

I discovered that I worked all the time first hand when I went to Hawaii with my family a few years back. As a side note, when entrepreneurs discover how to control their time they will get more time in Hawaii or whatever version of Hawaii you like. I am in Hawaii at least 4 times every year with my family.

Serious time management issues plagued my business back then. I realized this when at the end of my Hawaii vacation I had a fax bill of $175. This fax bill meant I had faxed over 1,000 pages during the 10 days I was there. Despite being in Hawaii and "on vacation" I was still working.

Working all of the time as an entrepreneur happens quite frequently because we have a passion for what we do. There is a time though when we have to turn it off, so we can recharge our batteries and spend time with those that support us in this crazy entrepreneurial world.

Firefighter Mentality

Firefighters work quickly and efficiently to put out fires.

Entrepreneurs can find fires where there shouldn't be fires. They are constantly getting into all aspects of their business and rushing to put out "fires."

A sure sign that you have this symptom of time management disease has to do with what you do first thing in the morning. Before you read further I would like you to answer one question for yourself:

What is the first thing that you do when you get to the office in the morning?

For many entrepreneurs the first thing that they do is they check their e-mail, voicemail, website orders, fax machine and anything that they can get their hands on that came in from the night before. Their day is dictated by their emails, voicemails, etc. that they receive in the morning.

This means that their days are never predictable. Every day turns into an adventure and is chaotic. They never have any time because their schedule is completely out of control. Each minute is spent fighting the next fire in their day.

When we look at it in detail, Firefighter mentality is actually a fear issue, not a time management issue. Entrepreneurs should spend their time doing $1,000 an hour work, not $10 an hour work. Getting faxes, checking voicemail, checking orders, and the issues that come in via e-mail can all be handled for $10-$15 an hour.

Entrepreneurs like to stay "busy." However, you have to stay busy with the right activities or your business will not grow.

Not Enough Money Making Activity

Allow me to be direct when I tell you the following: "When you aren't making the money you want right now, you aren't spending enough time on money making activities."

This may be the biggest sign that you have a time management problem. Before I get too far into this, allow me to define money making activity so we are on the same page:

"Money Making Activities for an Entrepreneur: Talking to prospects, running your marketing, coming up with new marketing, new strategies, and new products"

Outside of these activities, everything else can be delegated to someone who makes $10-15 an hour.

Entrepreneurs avoid money making, because for the most part they are control freaks. At the core they believe that no one can do it better than they can. While this may be the truth, when entrepreneurs adopt this strategy they are always stuck doing $10 an hour work and never have time to do $1,000 an hour work.

When entrepreneurs don't spend their time on money making activities, they limit the revenue growth of their company and put their livelihood at risk.

How much time do entrepreneurs spend on money making activities?

A few years back I surveyed my entire client base to find out how much time they were spending on money making activities.

The results shocked me. On average, my clients spent less than 30 minutes daily on money making activities. One of the most interesting things that I uncovered in the survey was that my clients were working an average of 65 hours a week.

They were working hard, just not smart. The time that they were spending was not on money making activities. This is a sign that you have a serious case of time management E.I.D.

Stop being an E.I.D entrepreneur and let's discover how we can be smart entrepreneurs who have their business under control.

Time Management Cures

The good news about time management is that it can be managed successfully to get you and your business to the next level.

Smart entrepreneurs, those that make the money they desire in less time, have traits and habits in common that take them to the next level. These traits are what have made my top clients my top clients.

Money Making Activity before Noon

Throughout this book I have outlined steps to get you to the next level. None may be as important at this point as getting your money making activity done before noon.

Regardless of your business, the money making activity needs to be done prior to noon on a daily basis. Remember the definition of money making activities is as follows:

"Money Making Activities for an Entrepreneur: Talking to prospects, running your marketing, coming up with new marketing, new strategies, and new products"

Over the years many of my clients have said to me the following: "Todd I am not a morning person, can't I do my money making activity in the afternoon."

My response is always, "No"!

First, I am not saying that you have to get up at 5:00 am and make cold calls. I am talking about running your marketing in the morning.

The main reason that the morning needs to be protected is that it is far easier to get your work done. In the morning, you can block off time and let your staff, business partners, and customers, know that work is being performed that is in their best interest. When entrepreneurs try and block off time in the afternoon it rarely happens.

In the afternoon, there will almost always be issues that require your attention. Attending to these issues will prevent you from doing your money making activity for your business.

Getting this right 100% of the time is asking for too much from entrepreneurs, so the goal is to get your morning, money making activities done correctly 80% of the time Monday through Friday.

Controlling the Phone

Recall that one of the biggest symptoms of E.I.D Time Management is controlling the phone. Getting control of the phone may require some serious counseling for some people; however this is critical to success

We already discussed how money making activities have to be done in the morning. So how does one control the phone and make sure that sales are taking place?

Many entrepreneurs run 100% of their calls through their cell phone. This creates challenges in controlling the phone. There are plenty of affordable ways to control the phone that I recommend to my clients.

One of my favorite methods of controlling the phone is an 800# that has tracking as one of the features. These numbers are extremely affordable. They allow prospects to call in and dial an extension which can provide information and then allow the prospect to get in touch with you. These systems provide tracking so you can see how your marketing is performing. When you are in your money making mode, you can simply set the sales extensions to forward to you and the support lines directed to others in your company.

Another system that works well is a system like Google Voice. This is a free service were you can get an additional phone number that will forward to your office or cell phone. This system will allow you to set the time of day that you will take calls, and it is as easy as clicking a few check boxes.

I put both of the above into my business. In the morning, it is virtually impossible to get me on the phone regardless of the number you have, unless it is a sales related call.

What I would like to suggest to you now is to choose at least one of the methods above to control the phone. Over time and trying out different methods you will discover the one that works best for you and your personality.

Price for Success

What would it feel like to know the exact number of hours you needed to spend on money making activities to hit your goals?

Hopefully, a feeling of security will rush over you when I reveal that you no longer have to spend the hours of 11:00 PM to 2:00 AM working on another draft of your business plan.

Part of managing your time as an entrepreneur comes from discovering just where all of this will take you. Many entrepreneurs fail to ever manage their time correctly because they can't put a quantifiable number on how many hours it will take to bring in the money they want to make, or how it will change their business.

A recent client said to me "Todd, I don't have time to work countless hours yet I really need to be successful. How much time do I need to put in on money making?"

The good news is regardless of what you have going on in the rest of your life or your business, the goal is 2-3 hours of money making activity prior to noon daily.

At every seminar, boot camp, and one on one consultation, I ask every audience and client the same question during our time together and that is the following:

"Would you like to make at least 1 million in net income if you didn't have work more hours than you are working today?"

99.9% of every client and audience member says yes. If you are still with me, allow me to share how this works out. Entrepreneurs tend to work longer, harder, and more often, yet not smarter. They don't do this intentionally. They do this because at their core they are willing to work for success.

I am here to tell you that making a 7 figure net income is about spending time on the right activities. Part of managing your time is discovering how to best spend your time. To reach your goals, 2-3 hours of money making activity is all that stands in your way.

When I say 2-3 hours of money making activity, I mean a full 2-3 hours. It isn't about taking 5 bathroom breaks, 3 coffee breaks, & 6 chats with your employees or coworkers. This is about focusing for short amount of time so you can reach the goals you have for your company.

By getting your money making activities out of the way in the morning, you will avoid afternoon distractions. For many entrepreneurs the afternoon isn't just about the distractions, it is about picking up kids, grocery shopping, and keeping in touch with friends. This is yet another reason why getting your money making activities done in the morning is so important.

But Todd…My Business Is Different
At every seminar I have ever conducted an attendee comes to me and says they can't do the 2-3 hours in the morning because their business is just so different, and their business wouldn't survive without them.

First, if you are an emergency room doctor you are excused from this discussion because your business is the health and safety of others.

For the rest of us, our business will eventually perish without us spending the 2-3 hours on money making activities. To be clear when an entrepreneur chooses to avoid spending 2-3 hours on money making their business will eventually die.

Now that we have removed the excuse of "my business is different", allow me to reveal more ways we can get time under control and avoid being an E.I.D entrepreneur.

Smart Entrepreneurs Steps for Success
To get over E.I.D we need to follow the path of successful entrepreneurs. The traits below are what successful entrepreneurs do on a daily basis. Let's dive into this so we can leave E.I.D behind.

Act like the Dr.

Dr's know how to run a model for effectiveness. They aren't reachable unless you are near death, and even then the nurse still tells you to head to the ER.

They spend their time doing money making activity all day long and in short, highly effective increments.

A Dr. doesn't hand out his personal cell phone number, answer it on weekends, and do all of the paperwork himself.

Dr's come in to see patients, ask them questions, make a recommendation, and then go on to see the next patient.

We all respect our doctors and aren't mad when they don't personally answer their phone to take our call. Acting like the Dr. will separate you from your competition and make it special to speak with you. The harder and more difficult it is to get in touch with you directly the more value customers will place on your time.

Acting like the Dr. will free up your time and ensure that the time you spend with your prospects is money making time, instead of just idle chit chat.

Another aspect of a Dr's model that I recommend will create time for the busy entrepreneur. The head nurse creates time in two ways for the entrepreneur.

A head nurse, like in a Dr's office, does all of the heavy lifting and makes sure the real work gets done. They see the patient first, they deal with the patient the most, and they keep the Dr. moving from patient to patient

The last benefit of the head nurse is one of the most important for entrepreneurs, so allow me to cover it first. Entrepreneurs, since they are their own bosses, become their worst enemies in managing their time.

Head nurses help to solve this problem by keeping you moving in the right direction. A quality head nurse keeps you from having meetings that run too long, spending time on your grocery list, and chatting with people who need to be working. They will move you on to the next task so that your business grows.

In regards to who should have a head nurse, and to what degree, allow me to share some numbers with you from my client base:

- 10% of clients have a full time head nurse
- 15% of clients have a head nurse 50% of the time
- 17 % of clients have a head nurse 25% of the time
- 8% of clients have a head nurse less than 15% of the time

50% of my clients have help in some area in their business. The 10% of my clients who have full time head nurses also make up the top 10% of my client base in net income. This is no accident as they are managing their time better than the rest.

Head nurses are great during regular business hours. I also encourage the use of answering services, just as Dr's have, when your office is not open. This will allow you to service your clients full time without you having to do it yourself.

The Power of 3

Years ago I discovered that 3 is an easy number to accomplish. Maybe this comes from helping real estate agents over the years that just wanted more 3% commissions. I find that 3 is very powerful because one can get 3 items done quickly and efficiently. 3 items can have a tremendous impact on their business.

Entrepreneurs often have to do lists of 42 different items. We all have these lists and they never get done. Smart entrepreneurs take their 42 items and limit it to 3 top daily goals.

Take your entire list and find 3 items that you are going to get done today. This may not seem like a large amount to accomplish on a daily basis. However, you will be getting 3 important task items done that will magnify the results of your business.

Controlling the Phone

As I mentioned, the phone is a gift and yet can be a curse to the entrepreneur. Controlling the phone will increase your income quickly.

This may take some fear management. However, I am going to ask you to change your voicemail message to indicate that you are going to return calls at two times during the day.

Each of my clients is different. However, most of them choose two times during the afternoon to return their calls. This allows them to get their money making work done before noon, which of course is money making time. Along with returning calls, I include returning e-mails. The same times that you return calls should also be used to return e-mails.

Just as I recommend a separate phone line for orders, I recommend a separate e-mail for sales orders so entrepreneurs can stay focused.

The goal is always to get as much work done as possible in the morning prior to returning calls. Having two times to return your calls also provides additional benefits.

It allows you to set time frames to accomplish your 3 important daily goals. When you allow yourself all day to accomplish a task you will take all day. When you allow yourself an hour to accomplish the task, you will figure out a way to get it done in 1 hour.

I would like you to keep in mind that even the biggest project can be broken down into 1 hour segments. Break it down, and get the pieces done, so you can reach your goals.

The Value of Time

Entrepreneurs who are successful know the value of their time. Right now I would like you to write down what you would like to make this year.

A typical example that an entrepreneur says to me is $100K. In order to make $100K you need to make $50/hr. This amount should be broken down so you can see it on a minute by minute basis.

Entrepreneurs who routinely do $10-$15 an hour tasks have a fear management issue in valuing their time. For now, I just want you to write down the amount you would like to make and break it down into an hourly basis. Put this number somewhere you can see it daily.

Outsource Everything

One cannot really outsource everything.   However, other than marketing and sales you should do everything you can to outsource tasks that take time away from sales and marketing.

This doesn't mean that you must have dozens of employees to make your business work. Having help can and should be a priority in your business. As an example, I have 47 different websites for the companies that I operate.

From graphics to SEO (Search Engine Optimization) to PPC Advertising (Pay Per Click) I have someone to help me do these tasks. Often times I get referrals from associates or partners. However, many times I have reached out to two websites. The two websites I use most often are www.Elance.com and www.Guru.com. Both of these sites allow me to hire help cost effectively for my businesses.

Your Assignment

To get to the next level with time management I have a few assignments that I am going to ask you to undertake.

The assignments for this week are as follows:

- Focus on money making activities before noon, Monday through Friday. This is 1-3hours a day. Try this just for one week, even if you have to tell your clients, employees, friends, and family that you are on vacation for the mornings that week. What you will discover is increased productivity, but you need at least 1 week to see the results.

- Tracking your conversations for 1 week. Write down on a notepad who you talk to, how long, and the subject of your conversation. This can be one of the most eye-opening

  Todd Bates Tip: Get sample time management charts that my clients use to get the most out of their days at: www.ToddBatesSystems.com /Resources

  of all of the tasks I have my clients perform. What you may discover is that your friends, family, even your loving spouse are the ones who are consuming a large portion of your day. Finding out who you are talking to, and what your conversations are about, will lead you to be able to uncover the biggest time wasters in your day.

- Organize your top 3 projects. Every entrepreneur, because of E.I.D, has dozens of projects. I want you to pick one of your projects, do it yourself and delegate the other two. You may end up delegating them to an employee, a consultant, or even a contractor. Get them done as cost effectively as possible, just get them done.

- Write down what tasks you get paid to do. Your job is to get new clients, however writing this down so you can see it every day, and the dollar amount you want per hour, will help guide the choices that you make on a daily basis.

Chapter 7 – Goal Setting For a 7 Figure Net Income

This is a chapter that I felt compelled to write as a part of this book. Over the years I have seen entrepreneurs attend many events and seminars related to goal setting. I myself have read a variety of books, and been at some of the same events with many entrepreneurs listening about setting and achieving our goals.

What I have discovered over the years is that 99% of people simply don't meet their goals. They start with the best of intentions. However, at the end of the year when they dust off their "plan" that they spent days, sometimes weeks preparing, they realize they missed their goals. Usually they didn't miss them by a little, but by a country mile. Their plan, that was to be the guiding force throughout the year, ended up being better used as a door stop than a goal setting device.

I am going to invite you to stop going to seminars on goal setting. Don't run to the book store and invest in a book on goal setting and business plans. You don't fit the mold that these books are speaking to. We are different because we suffer from Entrepreneurial Idiot Disease. This disease is what has prevented us from achieving our goals. When we can recognize that we don't fit the mold, we can approach goal setting from an entirely different perspective.

As you read through this chapter, I invite you to consider the sharpening the axe analogy. It's a story that you might have heard in some of the personal development circles. The story goes that you are given the task of chopping down a tree with an axe. You have just four hours to chop down this mighty tree.

The traditional entrepreneur takes the axe, runs full speed ahead and attacks the tree with zeal. No one can outwork this entrepreneur as he blazes ahead with bold indifference. He hacks away relentlessly and chops down the tree with just minutes to spare. He is tired, sweaty, and barely able to speak, but he has accomplished the goal, he chopped the tree down.

Meanwhile, the smart entrepreneur is just down the road. With the same time limit she examines her axe and realizes that it isn't sharp enough. She takes the next three and a half hours to sharpen her axe. Carefully, she sharpens the edges and gets it so sharp it can literally split a hair. With her blindingly sharp axe, she approaches the tree and chops it down in just 5 minutes.

Which entrepreneur do you want to be?

Let's have an honest conversation in this chapter. This is your time to sharpen your axe and to ensure that the next time you sit down to write your goals they will be achieved.

Crucial Points for Entrepreneurial Idiots To Embrace for Goal Setting

Entrepreneurial idiots are different than everyone else. We can't follow the same mold that they teach in business schools across the country. We march to a different beat, and often that beat sends us down the wrong path. When we can recognize our differences we can put goal setting in place that will help us not to merely set goals, but to achieve them.

The first crucial point that an entrepreneurial idiot should understand is that you can't set long term goals. Let me be clearer, you can set long term goals, but you won't reach them.

You can't stay focused long enough for goals that are long term. I want to challenge you to never set a goal that is longer than 30 days. Don't set 6, 12, and 18 month goals. Creating a plan to achieve key milestones in these time periods is an utter waste of time. It's a waste of time because you struggle with the disease.

Even smart entrepreneurs struggle with long term goals. They have already mastered time and fear management and yet it's still a challenge for them to reach long term goals. Make it easy on yourself to achieve success by only setting your goals 30 days at a time.

The next key point that most entrepreneurial idiots don't realize that prevents them from achieving their goals is that they never get specifically clear on the price they have to pay to hit their goal. This is one of the biggest reasons that most people set goals and fail to achieve them. To help you overcome this challenge, and get on the road to being a smart entrepreneur, I want to share with you my three times rule.

My three times rule states that everything you are trying to achieve will require a multiple of three. I want you to let this sink it. Any goal you are trying to achieve will take triple what you have in your mind. With a goal in mind I want you to think that hitting that goal will cost three times as much as you think it will. Your goal will require three times the energy. It will even take three times the amount of time!

Most entrepreneurial idiots don't hit their goal because they never get clear on the money, price, and time that it will take to hit their goal. The simple bottom line is that if you haven't hit your goal you haven't paid a big enough price. If you think it's going to take 30 days to hit your goal, get in your head it is going to take 90 days. If you think you can hit the next level in your business for an investment of $1,000, then you better get in your head it is going to cost you $3,000. No matter what goal is in your mind, make sure you are clear and honest with yourself about the three times rule. It is absolutely critical to get this right from the beginning.

The third critical point that entrepreneurial idiots should embrace on the road to being a smart entrepreneur is that they try to accomplish too much. Entrepreneurial idiot brains are running at 10,000 RPM's. We always have lots of ideas, numbers, and strategies running through our head. There is so much running through our minds that we get distracted and don't end up achieving our goals. To start hitting your goals, I will challenge you to slow your thought process down.

I want you to take a look at your to-do list. Most entrepreneurs' to-do lists are far too long! Have you ever had a list of 15+ projects that were all at about 82% completion? When you look through your list and absolutely none of your projects are at 100%, you surely have entrepreneurial idiot disease! The list is too long to accomplish anything.

The next crucial point has come as a shock to many of my clients. It shocks many entrepreneurs because they never thought about goal setting as a reflection of their passion. One of the key reasons that entrepreneurs don't hit their goals is because the goals they lay out are not in line with their true passion in life. Their goals don't align with their business, family, or even finances.

Entrepreneurs, who consistently fail to meet their goals, fail to understand the WHY behind their goals. In order to reach your goals you have to have a huge why! Let me share with you what happened at a recent seminar that can help you to understand your big why.

I was going through the goal setting exercise and I asked an attendee to share their big why. A lady raised her hand and she shared her goal of making $250,000 a year. When she shared that goal for her business she launched into a detailed description of how she would grow her business. She had a clear vision of what she could do to grow her business to the $250,000 a year level. After she had finished, I simply asked her "why" she wanted to achieve that goal.

She said that she wanted to get to that income level because she had a child going to college. He was going to be attending college in the next two years and she wanted to pay his way for the entire four years. Most attendees seemed happy with her answer. However, I challenged her to think deeper about her goals. I asked her what would happen if she didn't achieve her income goal. What would happen to her child's goal of going to college if she didn't make $250,000?

With little hesitation she mentioned that he would have to get loans and work his way through college. He wouldn't be any different from 90% of other college students. He would get his degree and have some debt to show for it. I then shared with her that it was unlikely she would achieve her goal. Her "why" wasn't big enough! Whether she accomplished her goal or not, her son would still be going to college. Quite simply, her why wasn't powerful enough, it wasn't big enough, it wasn't passionate enough. She didn't absolutely HAVE to make $250,000!

Let me be clear as this is what separates the entrepreneurial idiot from the smart entrepreneur. For most people, it would be nice to accomplish their goals, but they don't have to. Everyone wants to be rich, everyone wants to be in shape, everyone wants a great relationship, but do you really want it? Are you desperate enough?

The sad reality is that most entrepreneurs are too comfortable. When you are comfortable you won't make it to the next level. This process is about finding your real passion. When you can embrace being uncomfortable then you will be on the road to hitting your goals. It's not easy, change isn't easy, but that is what will free you from suffering with entrepreneurial idiot disease.

I went back to that client with her goal of $250,000. I wanted to find her real passion. I asked her what if your family couldn't eat if you didn't hit $250,000. What if you lost your home if you didn't hit your goal? What if you had to declare bankruptcy if you didn't hit your goal? I wanted her to dig deep to find her big why, a bigger why than simply providing college tuition for her son.

Most entrepreneurs simply aren't desperate enough. They don't have a big enough why to achieve their goals. Your challenge is to ask yourself what is your WHY. Embracing your why is critical as entrepreneurial idiots don't work out of inspiration, they work out of desperation. When you are comfortable you simply won't get to the next level. I need you to be desperate all the time. Desperation gets you to goals, while being comfortable will leave you wondering why, yet again, you are dusting off your "plan" at the end of the year.

A Smart Entrepreneurs Guide to Goal Setting

To help you cure yourself from entrepreneurial idiot disease I want to share with you a different way of goal setting. I want to reveal to you the key aspects of how smart entrepreneurs set goals. There are major differences that will require change. You could stick with how you are doing it right now, but remember it's not working! Hitting your goals doesn't mean more "focus" or buying a new business planner, it means changing your habits. To keep it simple I invite you to consider that smart entrepreneurs break up their goal setting into four parts.

Smart entrepreneurs write their goals down. You may have a clear vision of what is in your head. You may even wake up each morning and have a perfect understanding of what you want to achieve, but that's not good enough. Smart

Goal Setting Achievement Path

30 Day Goal

Weekly Goal

Daily Goal

Hourly Goal

Reward

Break down your goal to what you can do hourly to reach it. This makes your goal simple and easy to achieve.

- Todd Bates

entrepreneurs write their goals down and they make it as clear and specific as possible.

After you write down your goal, I want you to break it down. Your goal should be something that you can achieve in the next 30 days. It shouldn't be some long term goal like I want to be a millionaire by age 35, when you are 25 right now. People who suffer from entrepreneurial idiot disease can't handle long term goals because they lose focus. Making a goal that you can achieve in 30 days gives you an opportunity to break down the goal and achieve it.

Here is what I mean by breaking down your 30 day goal. Let's say your goal is to sell 10 of your product in the next 30 days. To sell 10 in a month would require a weekly goal of 2.5. With your weekly goal in mind, break that down to a daily goal, which means selling just ½ of a product daily. Even a daily goal of ½ can be too much for someone suffering from entrepreneurial idiot disease. Break your goal down further to what will happen in just a few hours. To sell ½ of a product daily might mean a certain number of prospects met, giving information to a certain number of people, making a certain volume of calls, etc. The point is to make your goal achievable by breaking it down to its smallest element.

Far too often people don't achieve their goals because they aren't sure how to get there. They write down a big goal (what some people call a "stretch" goal) and then they never write down how to get there. Having a big goal is great, but having no way to get to that goal is stupid. Breaking down your goals into smaller pieces where you aren't looking to go past 30 days will keep you hitting your goals every month.

The next part to goal setting for the smart entrepreneur is to ask yourself who is going to help you achieve your goal. Most entrepreneurial idiots rely solely upon themselves. The absolute worst thing you can do is to rely on yourself to achieve your goals. Some of you have been relying on yourself for 10, 15, even 20 years and where has that gotten you?

Relying upon yourself has gotten you into trouble, because the problem is you! Don't try to convince yourself that you can change or "this time" it will be different. Acknowledge your weakness and do what a smart entrepreneur does, identify who can help you achieve it. Be very honest with yourself. The bottom line is that if you knew what you were doing you would have gotten there already. Stop wasting time and get some help.

Writing your goal down and breaking it into smaller increments will help. Getting people to help you with your goal will allow you to get closer than you have ever gotten before. The sad reality is that if you don't get the next part right you will still miss your goal. I want you to understand the WHY behind your goal, and it needs to be big!

Your why should be so big it should almost feel overwhelming. Consider a why such as, I have to lose this weight or I will die. Or, maybe I have to make this money or I will lose my house. If your why isn't big enough you won't get to your goal. Once you have your why in place, write down the price you are willing to pay to get to your goal.

The price you are willing to pay isn't always just a monetary goal, although it might be. The price might be an amount of time. It might be an amount of energy. It might even be a price that involves time and money! Get the price written down and make it clear.

At a recent seminar I was going through my goal setting exercise. An attendee in the audience shared with the group that you should do a business plan instead of setting goals in the manner that I was sharing.

I asked this attendee what price he was willing to pay to achieve his goal. He said he was willing to pay $5,000 to accomplish his goal. After he shared that number, I asked him what if it cost him $15,000 (remember my three times rule)? He immediately spoke up and said, no way! I can't find $15,000, I don't have that kind of money, it just can't cost that much to get to my goal. I said, but if you did pay that $15,000, you would understand how to achieve that goal, how to pay the price, how to break a big goal down etc. He couldn't see it as he then went on to share with me a laundry list of reasons of why he couldn't do it.

My simple question to the rest of the audience was the following:

What do you think the odds are of him achieving this goal if he won't pay the price?

The short answer is he won't achieve his goal. He already has it in his mind that he isn't willing to pay the price! Be honest with yourself on the price that you are willing to pay. Be honest about the amount of energy, money, and time that it will take to get your business to the next level. Don't stop at saying a number or an amount of time, dig deep and ask yourself what if it was "3 times" that?

Relying on Motivation

One of the traditional mistakes is to mix goal setting with motivation. Many people set big goals and are confident they will get to them because they are motivated. They have a drive that most people don't see. They simply won't take "no" for an answer, so they will hit their goals, right?

Wrong.

Don't rely on your motivation level to hit your goals. I don't want you relying on your motivation level because motivation rises and falls on an hourly basis. We are business owners, sales professionals, and entrepreneurs and our mood swings hour by hour. You really shouldn't rely on your motivation level to achieve anything!

Just consider for a moment the process of weight loss. What do you think gives you a better chance to lose weight. Would you lose more weight by signing up and going to a trainer everyday at 8am or relying on yourself to go the gym? You end up losing more weight with the trainer because they are there in your face to make sure you do it.

When you are considering losing weight, the trainer becomes your system for success. In your business I want you to consider putting systems into place. Your marketing, your lead generation, and your goal achievement shouldn't rely upon you. If it does rely upon you it won't work. The smart entrepreneur understands that their motivation can change quickly. The smart entrepreneur won't allow themselves to fail so they put systems into action.

Systems are such an essential part of business. I want you to consider putting a reward system in place for yourself. With your reward at risk, keeping you reaching toward your goals is imperative. Most people fail to meet their goals because they don't stick with a system long enough to make it effective. Your reward system can be simple. I want you to come up with simple reward each time you achieve your goal. When you are hitting your goals hourly, reward yourself hourly. Hitting your goals weekly, reward yourself weekly. Remember the example I shared earlier with the business owner who needed to sell 10 products monthly. They would earn a reward every week they hit 2.5 sales. A simple reward system keeps your motivation level high and keeps you focused on your goals.

Warning! Don't Be Realistic

When you are defining your goals and creating your reward system, I don't want you to use the word realistic. Far too often when I am at live events and on coaching calls I have entrepreneurs share with me their goals, and before I can say anything they say "because that would be realistic."

In the past I used the word "realistic" until I came to the conclusion that what it really means is comfortable. I discovered I wasn't pushing myself whenever I wrote down a "realistic" goal. Entrepreneurs put realistic goals into action because it is a safety net. It is a method of fear management and it will leave you falling short of your goal. I am going to challenge you to be a goal setting maverick. Put down a bold goal, break it down, and start hitting your big goals.

Your Assignment

Goal setting requires change. Change will feel uncomfortable and that means you are headed in the right direction. Your assignment in this chapter involves six parts. Don't skip around, don't put the book down and say you will do it later, as those are symptoms of entrepreneurial idiot's disease. Start today and dive in with the following:

Todd Bates Tip: Get goal setting worksheets and share your goals at: www.ToddBatesSystems.com/ Resources

Identify Your Top 5 Goals For the Next 30 Days - Keep it to 30 days and keep it simple. I am not saying your top 15 items. I am not suggesting that you write a massive "to-do list." Write down your top five goals, keep them clear, and be specific.

Break Down Your Goals – Break down your top five goals into what that goal means weekly, daily and hourly. Don't cheat on this one. Break it all the way down to what you will need to do to hit your goals hourly and your monthly goals will happen fast.

Write Down Your WHY – Make sure your "why" is big enough. The bigger your why, the more likely you will hit your goals.

Write Down The Price You Will Have To Pay – Your price may be money. The price you are going to have to pay could be time. The price could be energy. When you write down your price revisit the three times rule. No matter what is in your head or how confident you feel, remember the three times rule.

Write Down Who – The road to recovery from EID means counting on other people. There is some sort of "who" who will be required to help get you to your goals. It might be a trainer or it might be someone from www.Elance.com. The bottom line is I don't want you relying on yourself to achieve your goals.

Reward System – Share with me your reward system. Don't give me your reward past one week. Your reward system should be regular, quick, and be on an ongoing basis. It should acknowledge that you are headed in the right direction.

Don't stay in the disease of goal setting! Get on the path to becoming a smart entrepreneur and tackle the six items here in this assignment. Some of you may (**hint**: everyone) need accountability. Take action now and share your goals and get more resources by visiting my website at www.ToddBatesSystems.com/Resources.

Chapter 8 – Bullet Proof System to Guarantee More Money Monthly

Entrepreneurs are notorious for having money issues. They make money and spend it. Often they spend it in the direction of their business. Everything becomes about growing the business to the point where they are often working for free.

Over the years I have had E.I.D with money management and I had to discover how to make sure my hard work showed up in my bank account. This isn't going to be advice that you have heard in a financial magazine, it comes straight from E.I.D experience. I want to make sure you don't have to face the issues I have had to, not to mention the 20,000 clients of mine who have had to face them, unless you really want to.

I want to be rich!

In all of the 2,243+ seminars, training events, and boot camps that I have conducted over the years, someone always comes up to me and says, "Todd, I want to be rich." People who say this are completely full of it. If they really wanted to be rich they would be.

I don't watch that much TV, however from time to time I turn it on to see what is going on in the world. Reality TV provides a glimpse of the "I want to be rich" crowd. They are living the life that most people believe the rich live. Unfortunately, I have read how many of these so called "rich" individuals on these shows are actually bankrupt or near bankruptcy.

If they really wanted to be rich they would be. This isn't to say that you can't achieve wealth. The pursuit of just "wealth" and "riches" rarely, if ever, works because you aren't following your passion.

The issue of money management is one that most entrepreneurs don't like discussing because it makes them uncomfortable. Comfortable people don't make changes. When you are uncomfortable you will make changes, take action, and get results.

Bottom line on money management is that if you don't have the money you desire now, you haven't paid a high enough price and it is your fault. When I don't have the right amount of money in my bank account, it is my fault as well. We all must take responsibility for where we are right now so we can move forward to the next phase.

I will share with you how I was financially secure for myself and my family by the age of 32. Just as a quick reminder, I didn't have any family money, I am not a genius, and I didn't take a company public. So wherever you are with the money you have now this chapter will put more money in your pocket.

Let's look at symptoms of money management so we can identify where we are and what we have to do to get to the next level.

How much do you really make?

Pick up a magazine about entrepreneurship and they will tell you how entrepreneurs are running companies that have 3.5 million in sales. The question I always have is "How much is the owner actually making?"

Most entrepreneurs have cash flow, yet very little net income. A client of mine ran a consulting group. Consulting is a high profit business and hers was running at 1.7 million or so in sales. She came to me for help because she "had no money."

She had employees, office space, machines, travel expenses (99% under estimate what travel will cost) accounts that were delinquent, and costs of keeping credit balances. On the surface she had a great business that was doing well. When I asked her what the biggest issue in her business was she said, "I am finding it difficult to pay my mortgage."

Her mortgage was not $20K monthly, it was extremely affordable. She had massive cash flow, however no real net income in her business. This is not unusual for entrepreneurs. They make sure others get paid while they continue to wait. She was not focused on her net income and that is the first symptom of a management problem.

Fighting an uphill battle from the beginning

Many entrepreneurs are fighting an uphill battle with their business from the start and they don't even know it. They have too little funding to get their business off the ground and spend their entire careers just chasing money.

As I mentioned earlier, over the years I have helped thousands of real estate agents. Real estate agents as a group are notoriously underfunded. They scrape together enough money to take their classes, get their license, and pay a minimum office bill. The total investment amounts to less than $2,000 in most cases.

97% of all real estate agents tell me their goal is to make $100,000. In general, they have very little money to spend on marketing. They are continuously chasing the only business they can afford, which is referral business. They never get out of survival mode because they start out with no funding. You don't have to have tons of money to invest in your business; however you do have to have capital.

For all of those waiting to "get money" and then spend it, you will keep waiting. When you desire to succeed you will find money, so stop waiting.

10,000 lbs of Debt

Debt can be a weight that cripples an entrepreneur. Just over 87% of the business owners who seek my help as their marketing coach have debt. Virtually 100% of them have two items in common when it comes to their debt:

1. They do not know how much debt they have and the details of their debt.
2. They have no plan on how to pay off their debt

I don't want you to be in debt. Scraping by, just to pay debt and barely make an actual living, can be extremely frustrating and stressful.

If you have debt right now you are not alone. The first thing to know is that you are in debt and how much. Later I will share with you a plan on how to get out of debt.

4 Biggest Money Management Issues

There are 4 big money management issues that entrepreneurs face. These four may be the biggest hurdles that prevent entrepreneurs from reaching their goals.

Attitude

The phrase that I hear at every seminar is the following:

"I don't have money to spend on marketing"

This is not a money management problem. When someone says this it is a fear management problem. When someone tells me they will do something once they have money, I know they won't make it until they overcome their fear of going broke.

When someone really wants to succeed they will find the money. They will sell something, work an extra job, or borrow from family to get the money they need to invest in marketing.

Attitude is more than just the thoughts one has towards money. Our attitude toward ourselves can directly affect how much money we make.

I have a client who's a professional body builder. This man is a physical specimen of a human being. He has spent years working-out, watching his diet, and studying to perfect his body. He is also a mortgage broker, which is why he contacted me.

The confidence that he displayed in his body building didn't exist in his mortgage business. His lack of confidence was affecting everything he was doing. His lack of confidence caused him to risk almost no money on marketing, which just made him less money. As a result of his attitude, he was continuously in survival mode.

Do you believe in yourself?

Your attitude and belief in yourself will directly affect the money in your bank account.

Laziness

The majority of entrepreneurs are not lazy; however I do run into some who are just outright lazy. At the live events that I conduct I always run into business owners who are trying to make as much money as possible without working.

They are chasing the "Internet Dream" of sitting behind their computer and making money. I have a few clients who make over 7 figures a year on the internet, and they work hard to make it happen.

Let's get this right out in the open; we call it work for a reason. It isn't about working 2 hours weekly and making $100K a year. When someone is lazy they never have money as they chase every get rich quick scheme in existence.

Laziness will always lead to poor money habits.

Self Discipline Issues

On a recent plane flight a fellow business traveler was complaining about their lack of money. In the next sentence she commented to me "I hate working from home, I can only work after the soap operas are over." This woman was dead serious about watching her TV shows.

Entrepreneurs who have self discipline problems would rather be doing something else. They focus on anything other than work. It ranges from doing grocery shopping during the day to hanging out with friends for 2 hour lunches. They enjoy the "freedom" of owning their own business and complain about the money aspect.

They may also have a hard time hiring the help they need and of course managing their money.

We all have self discipline issues to some degree, and knowing that this is part of our personality will make it easier to manage.

Working at this is a daily task and daily effort. For money management and self discipline to work we have to agree that you are either moving forward or moving backward. An entrepreneur cannot be satisfied with standing still.

A recent client of mine said "Todd, I just want to keep sales where they are." That is the same as going on vacation but saying "I just want to stay home."

You can't have a successful business without it growing. If you are standing still you are moving backward. Every year prices increase on everyday items, so the quicker you commit to growing your bottom line the better your business will be.

Your business doesn't have to grow at 300%, (although I would say that is a good idea) however it does have to grow in order to survive and thrive in any economy.

Fear Management

You may be afraid of what may or may not happen. Fear of losing money and even the fear of making money may be holding you back.

One of the key issues clients face is the fear of making too much money, and what they would do when they reach their goals.

Right now I would like you to look at your attitude toward money and identify with the one, two, or maybe three or more symptoms you have that are preventing you from succeeding financially.

Solving Money Management

The great news about what I am going to reveal about money management is that #1, everyone can begin to do it immediately and #2, its simplicity is what makes it so powerful.

The system that I have developed has 3 key components that make up the system. Break any of the 3 rules and you will not be managing your money effectively. On the bright side, there are only 3 rules. 3 rules separate you from financial success.

3 Rules That Will Change Your Financial Life

1. Stop Lying to Yourself
2. Understanding the Real Numbers Around Your Life & Your Business
3. Bank Account System

Let's get into the details of these rules and how they will change your financial future forever.

Stop Lying To Yourself

Just to be clear, we all lie to ourselves when we are having money issues. Years ago I was lying to myself, and I have seen countless attendees and even clients lie about their situation. I even had a couple of clients who were partners and one of them would get "sick" every first of the month because of their financial issues. They hid this from me for over 12 months as they were in complete denial about their financial situation.

What I would like you to do right now is to be honest with yourself. Wherever you are right now I can promise you someone else is worse off than you are. I know individuals who were making $500K on a monthly basis and went broke.

There isn't an amount of money that can't be outspent, and really there isn't an excuse that cannot be made to avoid finding out the truth. As the saying goes "the truth hurts." The time to act is now, not next week or even next month.

Understanding the Real Numbers in Your Life & Business

Entrepreneurs tend to avoid the details in their business because they aren't detail oriented and they aren't focused on the bottom line. Understanding the numbers you are facing will give you a clear path to success.

A story from my early days will shed some light on why identifying the numbers will lead you to the conclusion you need to take.

Out of college I was well over $50,000 in debt. Keep in mind that my GPA was not one that you would want to put on a resume. I have shared my GPA with every live audience I have ever been in front of. It was a stellar 1.7.

When your GPA is below 2.0 your choice is to start serving food or go into sales. My choice, if you haven't guessed, was sales.

My first business was the real estate business. For the first 90 days I struggled. To be honest, I just kept getting deeper into debt. The next step I took is the opposite of what most people choose to do. I hired a coach to help me. This coach cost me $2,500 a month. Within 12 months I was completely out of debt. By the end of my second year in real estate I had a very high 6 figure net income. In my third year out of college I had a 7 figure net income. Every year since my third year out of college I have had a 7 figure net income regardless of the economy.

You might be able to picture a slightly cocky, confident 25 year old who was making 7 figures. I thought I was pretty hot stuff to say the least.

My coach and his group lived in Oregon and I knew they made 1 million a month, while I made 1 million a year. Needless to say I wanted to play in their world. When I met with them in Oregon one of my coach's associates asked me the following question:

"Todd, how many times have you gone bankrupt?"

When I answered that I have never been bankrupt, he told me to come back only after I had been bankrupt 3 times. Their attitude (not one that I would recommend) was that if you haven't gone bankrupt you aren't serious.

There is a price to pay for success. Their price was bankruptcy. I would say you don't have to go into financial ruin to succeed; however failing to know your numbers could put you in bankruptcy if you aren't careful.

Know the real numbers in your life. The following questions are what I have every client ask themselves:

- How much do you need for your lifestyle?
- How much do you need for your business?
- What are your total debts for business and personal?

The most important business questions that every entrepreneur needs to have the answers to are the following:

- How much they make per client?
- How much a client is worth on average?
- How much their marketing costs are, on average?
- How long does it take for you to get a client?

The answers to these questions will put money in your pocket and guide the decisions you make. By understanding the numbers, a business owner can separate themselves emotionally from certain decisions.

I had a client who had an online business selling niche motorcycle parts. On average, he made $143 per client. He was contemplating running a magazine ad to drive additional traffic to a portion of his website. The cost of the magazine ad meant he had to generate 15 sales from the ad just to break even. His long term value of his customers made it worth it, provided he could break even on the ad.

When he ran the ad he generated 20 sales. Because he knew his numbers he kept running the ad. Recently the ad performance dropped to the point where he was only generating 12 sales. Even after modifications to the ad, the performance was not enough to cover the cost of the ad.

Knowing the numbers, he was able to cancel the ad even though he loved it. This means he is not wasting money on advertising that isn't working, which is critical to success.

95% of the clients whom I ask these questions don't know the answers. Knowing the answers to the questions above is critical to money management.

E.I.D Bank Account System

This is a system that I was taught, and have since perfected. It will change the way you manage your money, and by just following a very simple process, will increase your net income. All of my clients who are serious about their success follow this system.

The first part of the bank account system is to understand, it happens on a weekly basis. Entrepreneurs are notorious for looking at their numbers on a monthly basis. This doesn't provide enough time to make corrections to what is occurring in your business.

Every Friday, across all of my businesses, I add up all of the income that has come in for the week. For businesses that I have partners in, we agree that all money is totaled up on a weekly basis.

5 separate transfers make the system work. For all of the money that comes in, I have 5 transfers that take place. To make things easy, I have 5 bank accounts and the percentage I associate with each one are as follows:

- Taxes - 20%
- Savings - 20%
- Lifestyle - 25%
- Debt reduction - 20%
- Cash account - 15%

By following this system I avoid the issues that many entrepreneurs face. A recent client of mine who makes just over $50,000 a month called me because he couldn't pay his taxes. He was failing to save on a monthly basis for taxes and was facing a huge tax bill.

In my businesses I don't have this issue and always have access to additional funds for new opportunities. One of the most important accounts is the debt reduction account. Wherever you are, having a plan to pay off all of your debt is critical to success. Once your debt is paid off this money can be used for whatever you desire.

I have clients who donate 20% of their monthly income to various charities that are dear to them because they have achieved their goal of being debt free by following this system.

This system runs every Friday in all of my businesses. Every Monday my bank accounts all show $0 which means I have to get to work. The majority of business owners work best from desperation not motivation so having $0 in your bank account will be very motivating.

Your Assignment

E.I.D money management is one that that can be mastered in days provided you are willing to undertake a few short assignments.

When someone tells me they are having financial issues the assignment below is what I give to

Todd Bates Tip: Money management can be solved this week provided you take action:
www.ToddBatesSystems.com /Resources

them. I would invite you to tackle these 3 assignments this week without delay.

1. **Stop making excuses**. Excuses will only make things worse, so stop making excuses immediately so you can move forward.
2. **Get a clear vision of where you are.** How much debt? What are your expenses?
3. **Put the multiple account system to work**. Set-up the required accounts this week so you can begin to put the power of the accounts to work in your favor.

Right now, wherever you are, I need to ask you to take 100% responsibility for where you are. It is time to own up to your situation, good or bad, so you can move forward from where you are.

Living on a budget is relative, when using the bank account system you will discover the more money you make the more you get to live on. My lifestyle has never suffered it has only improved as a result of following this system.

I look forward to hearing how you put it to work on your behalf.

Chapter 9 – How to Take the Next Step in Your Business

Along our journey together through this book my goal is that you have discovered a little bit about yourself and even more on how you can get to the next level in your business.

As a reminder, when I ask every entrepreneur at my live events "would they like to get to the next level?" the answer 100% of the time is YES, and I hope it is for you as well. What the next level looks like depends on the vision that you have for your company and your life.

Let's look at the challenges that prevent E.I.D entrepreneurs from becoming the vision they have for themselves.

Managing Your Fears

Managing your fears must be done on a daily basis and in some cases on an hourly basis. Of all of the categories, failure to manage this one correctly will prevent the entrepreneur from getting out of survival mode.

Fear management is one that we all share in common. There isn't a single entrepreneur who doesn't have the fear of success, fear of going broke, and even the fear of what others think of them. After having conducted thousands of training sessions I still care about what others think of my presentation and me at the end of the day.

Those who conquer E.I.D discover that it is a day to day process to manage their fears and refuse to allow fears to hold them back. Keep in mind that managing the fear that is holding you back today doesn't mean that another one won't sneak up on you tomorrow. I am not suggesting that you live your life in fear; however it means we acknowledge that being a successful entrepreneur has challenges and we must be prepared to face them on a daily basis.

Uniqueness

In a world where everyone sounds the same and has a message like "I am honest, use me!" you are willing to step outside the box.

Crafting a marketing message is the cornerstone upon which you will build your business empire. Looking at the different categories that are available to you, which one stands out?

Do you feel called to hang your hat on one of these categories?

Nobody goes to the ice cream store to buy vanilla so the key is to step outside your comfort zone with your message. Be bold, be over the top, and use the message everywhere so prospects will be beating down your door.

It requires a bit of fear management to create a powerful marketing message, so take a moment to craft one that forces your business to succeed.

Time Management

In the world of being an entrepreneur this one has no cure. The good news is this is treatable and we can succeed.

The goal of time management should be to allow yourself to focus on what grows your business the fastest, which is $1,000 an hour work. All of the strategies, techniques, and methods that I shared with you about managing your time will allow your business to get to the next level provided you put them into action.

Sales Conversion

No one likes a salesman, especially a pushy one. The less you look like a salesman the better your business will do. Many of my clients even put the phrase "Don't look like a salesman" in a place where they can see it every day and on every phone call they make.

With sales and conversion the goal is to sound like a consultant. Consultants always make more than salesman and they are well respected. Looking at your business, how can you sound more like a consultant? What answers do your customers desire? How can you ask them questions to reveal that you are their trusted advisor, not just some salesman trying to hawk them some product they don't need.

Goal Setting

E.I.D entrepreneurs set goals that never get accomplished until they discover how to set goals correctly. Annually they meet, plan, and write out goals that get stuck in a folder they never look at till the following year.

Entrepreneurs need to have a big why first? What is your big why?

After figuring out your big why, take your goals and break them into 30 day goals, then weekly, and then daily goals.

Goals need to be set to grow our business, not to be set and thrown in a folder. Look at the activities that will grow your business and how much of these activities need to be done in order reach your goals.

Money Management

Remember to play the money management game based on your personality. Avoid being the entrepreneur who has a huge gross income yet no net income. It is about having enough money to pay your taxes, live your lifestyle, and keeping you motivated on a daily basis.

Managing your money correctly will give you the freedom, power, and ability to make the choices that are in the best interest of you and your business. You will forever avoid making the decision that is for today and you will make the best decision for your future.

Regarding money, you set the rules to the game so play the game to win!

Bottom Line

As I have mentioned throughout this book I can be counted on by my clients to give them a direct, no nonsense bottom line answer to their questions. The bottom line with all of this is to pick one of the items from the above list.

E.I.D entrepreneurs will try and tackle the entire list at one time and never finish. It will end up in pile of "To Do's" that never get done. The first step to overcoming your E.I.D, now that you have made it this far, is to pick one from the list above and tackle it.

Which one you pick from the list is up to you. Some will pick the one they feel is the hardest for them, while others the easiest.

The choice is yours; however the key is that you pick one for success.

Enjoying the Journey

Over the years many of my clients became so obsessed with the destination and vision in their head they failed to enjoy the journey. As entrepreneurs, part of what makes us unique and different is the process of building.

I would like to ask you to enjoy the journey you are on regardless of where you are now. Each point, even the low ones, has something you can use to get you to the following day and yes the next level.

Along your journey I look forward to hearing from you. Please share with me your journey, your progress, and your challenges. Throughout this book I have mentioned a specific portion of my website where I share information which you can use to grow your business. I would invite you to visit www.ToddBatesSystems.com/Resources and join me and others to help you grow your business.

To your success,

E-mail: Todd@toddbatessystems.com

Cell Phone: 303-841-8008

Resources for 7 Figure Net Income Entrepreneurs

In this book I have mentioned various resources that will help you avoid E.I.D. These resources have been used by me, my companies, and by my clients. At the online resource center for this book at www.ToddBatesSystems.com/Resources I have put together additional resources such as the cheat sheets and guides I have mentioned.

I would invite you to put these resources to work on your behalf. As time goes on, the online resource will be updated with the latest tools and information to help you avoid E.I.D. Where possible I have put the websites in categories so you can scan down the list to find the resource that matches up with your immediate need.

When you explore the online resources, I have special bonuses to help you avoid E.I.D that are not included in this resource section.

Help for the Entrepreneur

Every entrepreneur who is getting over their E.I.D needs help in their business. You may not need a full time assistant, yet however getting some help is critical to your success.

www.Elance.com – I have used this site and continue to do so for help. Individuals on this site offer a variety of services. Personally, I have hired graphic designers, copywriters, and web designers from this site. I use their escrow feature on every job that I hire someone for.

www.Guru.com – This is another website that I have used to hire graphics and administrative support. Many of my clients use this site to find affordable help for their businesses.

E-mail Auto responders

A well written auto responder is like having 6 full time employees. There are hundreds of these products on the market. Below are several I have used in the past or continue to use. Where possible I have noted the price range of the service as well. More detailed information on these products is available in the online resource center for this book.

www.GetResponse.com – Considering the price of this auto responder, is under $20 a month, it is extremely powerful. Many of my clients run substantial businesses off of this product. It may not have the bells and whistles of other sites, however for the price it is great tool to have in your business.

www.ConstantContact.com – This is another auto responder service that is under $20 a month. They have a variety of features that make it easy to use and to stay on top of your prospects.

www.Infusionsoft.com – My businesses run on this e-mail software. It is truly more than e-mail and the power allows you to look, act, and feel like you have a large team supporting your business. My average client whom uses this software saves hiring 1-2 full time employees. This software itself costs a few hundred dollars on a monthly basis. On the surface this may look expensive until you consider the savings from hiring additional staff.

Online Conferencing

Whether you have a pure online business or a brick and mortar business, reaching out to your customers via conference lines is a great way to increase sales.

www.Xiosoft.com – I have used this company ever since it began offering the service of online seminars. The software is easy to use and doesn't require the installation of software. My clients enjoy the easy to use features such as recording calls, web pages for each call, and ability to upload audio clips. They have a variety of products and I have used most of them. The price for the online conference is around $50 a month.

www.FreeConferenceCall.com – Free is great. This service is free and also allows you to record the calls that you conduct. It has a few limitations on the number of callers and conference time allowed. However this is a great place to get started when doing online seminars.

www.GoToMeeting.com - This product is one that has an array of features and power. Considering the price starts at $50 and has limited functionality this is only for those who conduct a large number of online training, sales, or information events on a monthly basis.

Websites

The Internet isn't going anywhere so if you don't have a website you are missing out. The good news is you don't have to spend big money to get started. The resources below will help any entrepreneur get started. You can always find help using the resources below in the "Help for Entrepreneurs" section.

www.Weebly.com – Get started with a free website. Many of my clients don't have a website and this is a great place to get a nice looking and professional website started.

www.WordPress.com – Blogs are really just websites when you get down to it. Having an easy to update website is great for the busy entrepreneur. I personally update my websites with content on a weekly basis only because they are on a Wordpress platform. It is as easy as typing on a computer once it is set up. Running your website on a Wordpress platform can be free to very low cost.

Online Advertising

Having a website is great however without a way to generate new business it will fall flat. Traffic is critical to your success; however keep in mind that it is about leads and not traffic.

www.Google.com/Ads - Advertising on Google is easy to start. With Google advertising finding your niche is critical. When you need help with your Google advertising I recommend finding someone who has certification through Google. The consultants who help me are both certified and have spent their own money and continue to do so with Google.

www.Yahoo.com & www.Bing.com – Yahoo and Bing (formerly www.MSN.com) are still players in the online advertising game. Each search engine has different types of visitors. Some of my clients find their most profitable traffic comes from Yahoo in comparison to Google. Testing and tracking are important regardless of which search engine you select.

www.Facebook.com – Social media is one of my favorite platforms. The majority of the activities are free, yet they require us to take action on them. True entrepreneurs who avoid E.I.D make it a system. Advertising on Facebook can generate leads very quickly. Watch your budget and results carefully.

Phone

Phones can be either a tool or a handicap to the entrepreneur. With the tools below you will make the phone a powerful tool in your business.

www.PhoneTag.com – This is a service that I have used for years. I hate voicemail and this service transcribes all of my calls. You save hours by not checking your voicemail and when the call can be handled by your assistant it is easy to forward the message since it comes transcribed to your e-mail.

www.Google.com/Voice - Google now offers the ability to get a new phone number where everything gets transcribed. The great part is you can forward the number to any existing phone and schedule the times that you receive calls. This increases your productivity and keeps you from being an E.I.D entrepreneur.

www.Proquest-tech.com – Having an 800# with tracking will allow any entrepreneur to see what is working and what is not with their marketing. Tracking and reporting are everything when you want to know what is effective and what is not generating a return on your investment. For years I have used this service with all of my companies and continue to do so. The service is around $50 a month for a phone number and 999 extensions.

For additional resources I would invite you to visit the online resources for this book at www.ToddBatesSystems.com/Resources.

Discover Systems to Prevent E.I.D and Increase Your Business 4X

The information that follows is new to this updated version of the book.

What you will discover is additional articles and information that have been published since the original release. These articles and additional information will help you increase your business regardless of economic conditions.

At any time throughout these articles I encourage you to call me direct at 303-841-8008.

To your success,

Todd Bates

Direct: 303-841-8008

Why E-mail Sucks for 99% of Business Owners & 4 Strategies to Improve Your Response Rates

Do you have an email newsletter you are sending out? When you have inventory that you want to move do you rush to your computer to send out a "blast" email? Have you noticed that the response rates on your emails have dwindled compared with a year ago? Is email a KEY part of your overall marketing strategy?

Increasing mail costs and the ease of putting email into action has increased the volume of emails that people receive 10 fold. As most business owners see it there is no "cost" associated with emailing. After all, you are already paying the bill for your server; why not send out a few thousand emails? Tragically most business owners will send out emails and barely hear back from their customer base. You could literally give away the store and you might not hear hardly a word because your prospects found it easier to click "Delete" than it was to actually read your email.

The majority of emails get deleted or marked as spam simply because people are following bad advice or making common mistakes that can be fixed in minutes. To jump start your results today, I invite you to consider the following email marketing methods.

1. Interest Piquing Subject Line – Far too often the subject line dooms the email. Just envision your email inbox and 60% of the messages have something related to "free" or "greatest deal" in the subject line...those are doomed to get deleted. When you want your message

to stand out it is essential to have a subject line that makes it irresistible for people NOT to take action. This comes down to identifying what is most important to your customers (time, money, value, etc) and avoiding the spam filters at the same time.

2. Vary Your Email Styles – Only sending emails where you are asking them to make a purchase will get you marked in the "follow up later" pile. Using email marketing for your business means creating emails that add value, tell a story, share a testimonial, and pique interest. Let those that are in your database know you are there for more than just selling them your product/service.

3. Length of Follow Up – Sending an email every now and then or when you have a sale isn't enough. Improving your response rate means having an email marketing plan that follows up with people for 90 days, 180 days, even over a year. Optimally you have different email follow up sequences for those who invest in your product compared to those who haven't.

4. Make it Obvious on HOW to Take Action – Each email should have a goal. Give people an option to call you, email you back, or revisit your website. Don't confuse them by giving them all 3 options in a single email; just make it clear on what you want them to do.

When you can create interest piquing subject lines, vary your email styles, have a long follow up sequence, and make it clear and obvious on HOW a prospect can take action then you will be in the top 1% of business owners getting the most from their email marketing.

Discover how to make email a part of your marketing systems with my FREE Marketing Manifesto below. When you want more direct help or you are just tired of watching endless videos and reading reports, call me direct, on my cell phone at 303-841-8008 and I will share with you a direct solution for your email marketing today.

How to Develop a Follow Up Process that Increases the Return on Your Marketing Strategy

When you put in a complete marketing strategy for your business you should be receiving leads daily. Prospects interested in finding out more, possibly comparing your prices to a competitor, or maybe they just have a question about what is possible. Regardless of the inquiry each lead is an opportunity to generate a sale or for some business owners to lose a sale.

Just think for a moment all of the items that are presented to you each day. From doing a search on Google, logging in to Facebook and even your drive into work. How many ads and distractions are you presented with? Now combine those distractions with the events of your life (kids, dry cleaning, vacation, etc). Do you sometimes forget about a particular task or action item?

The MASSIVE volume of distractions in today's world makes it necessary for more detailed follow-up. Making a few calls (or even emails) and hoping your prospects take action will only result in them taking action elsewhere. To cut through distractions, pique interest, and give your prospects an opportunity to take action means having a detailed follow-up process as part of your overall business marketing strategy. Consider the following elements involved JUST for follow-up:

- **Email Campaign** – An auto responder email campaign can cover, 60, 90, or even 300+ days of follow up to give the prospect valuable information and give them an opportunity to reach out to you right when they want to buy.

- **Postcard follow up** – With dwindling mail volumes you can grab their attention at the end of their day. A quick, cheap postcard can give them another opportunity to take action.
- **Phone calls** – Scripts on calls should be balanced for both leaving messages and live conversations. A call schedule should be put in place for each type of lead to ensure no opportunities are missed.
- **Direct Mail Pieces** – This could be catalogues, a newsletter, or even a questionnaire.

The more detailed your follow-up process the better return you will yield on your lead generation activities. Call me direct at 303-841-8008 with any questions.

How Are You Marketing to Affluent Prospects?

When you think of marketing to affluent prospects, what first comes to mind? Do you think of the big brands that have had massive successes such as Rolex, Ferrari, and Coach? While these brands have defined themselves in the luxury segment, unless you have 10's of millions laying around to invest in building a brand, trying to model after their success will just result in you throwing away your hard earned money.

Creating a marketing strategy for the affluent prospect, while it has many components, can be boiled down to 2 key aspects.

1. Your Marketing Message
2. Your Marketing Materials

Those who make over $500,000 a year have the same goals as many people: Save Time and Save Money. The challenge is that in order to reach these prospects, your message better be LASER focused to reach them as they value their time more than most people (that's why they are successful). Just think for a moment, how closely a Dentist, Surgeon, and Lawyer book their appointments. This group of professionals understands that their time is valuable and when you can reach to them with an opportunity to achieve their goals (especially with the option of saving time and money) you will have marketing that brings in the prospects that you truly desire.

Reaching this target market can't be done with the same tired marketing materials that most people use. Now, don't get me wrong you don't have to go over the top with high-glitz imagery, videos and more, but you do HAVE to make it professional and EASY for someone to achieve their desired goal.

Just think for a moment if you went into the Doctor's waiting room and there was trash around the chairs, it smelled funny, and the pictures on the wall were faded. Would you have the confidence that that Dr would pay attention to your needs in detail?

When you are looking to pursue the affluent market consider creating a cohesive set of materials for your small business marketing strategy that allows people to understand your unique value and easily contact you. Just consider some of the following marketing materials:

- Website
- Twitter Page
- Facebook Fan Page
- Brochure(s)
- Email Templates
- Postcards

You could waste countless hours trying to figure this out on your own or even spend 10's of thousands in the wrong direction. To save you time in your goal of reaching the affluent market I invite you to consider two options.

Call me direct on my cell phone – **303-801-8008** – I will outline the shortcut of how you can reach the affluent market, regardless of how your niche. This is my cell phone, be prepared for a direct conversation on how to put it into action quickly.

3 Methods to Generating More Leads, Calls, and Sales with Video Marketing

Are you using video as part of your marketing strategy on Facebook? Are you sharing videos on YouTube? YouTube shared that only 1 user per 1,000 is actually uploading video content. Anyone who isn't uploading video is merely an audience member while those who share video are the ones controlling the station!

Whether you like video, hate it, or are indifferent there is little doubt that video will continue to play a larger role in business and entertainment. With Google enabling TV's to easily watch YouTube and Facebook spreading videos wildly through the News Feed (hey who doesn't love Cats) now is the time to put video to work for your business. While it may not be possible to have a kitten demonstrate your product on an iPad, we invite you to consider the following video marketing strategies to get the most from your efforts.

1. **Ask Your Audience to Take Action** – In video you can speak to your audience. Your video doesn't need to be an infomercial with the hard sale; you can invite your audience to take an action that doesn't require a credit card. As you are sharing value, piquing interest, and engaging your audience ask them to "like" your video (when on Facebook) or ask them to give you a "thumbs up" on YouTube. By asking your audience to take action in the video you can increase interactions and get more exposure. Of course you can take it a step further (mixing it up in video is important) by inviting them to call you, email you, and yes take action by investing in your product/service.

2. **Include Video in a Blog Post** – When you have someone's attention, keep them even more engaged with your copy. Write a blog post that complements your video. You can share tips that aren't in the video, and give prospects one more opportunity to take action. By using your video in a blog post it can dramatically increase the time a user stays on your site; getting you closer to the sale.

3. **Remind People of Your Video Through Email** – Videos can have a short lifespan (there is always a cuter kitten). Get more from your video marketing efforts by including reminders to watch your videos in your auto responder sequence. It can be a short email like "hey thought you would like this video…" Keep it simple and let people know you have more value to share on your YouTube channel or on Facebook.

When you ask your audience to take action, include videos in your blog posts, and even remind them in your auto responder to watch your videos you will be able to generate more leads and sales with your video marketing efforts.

Sales Letters and Testimonials, 1 Trick to Improve Your Conversion Rate

The majority of people don't want to be "first" to try something new. Yes, there are a few brave souls who are pioneers and push the envelope in business and exploration but they are the minority. Most people when they consider a product or service want to know that other people have tried it. If people in their own sphere of influence haven't tried it, how do they know it will work?

People don't want to waste time, money and energy "trying" something just to have it fail! When you are sending out our sales letters for your product or service your prospects have doubt. Your sales letter might be well crafted, might assuage some of their fears, and by the time they make it to your call-to-action they might just throw it in the trash can. It lands in the trash can because they aren't confident enough about what you are offering.

Most sales letters lower the fear by using some or all of the following elements.

1. Time limiting offer
2. Unbelievable Pricing
3. Powerful Calls to Action

While these methods and more should be used, it still leaves you more opportunity to reach your prospects. You can remove more doubt from the prospects mind and compel them to take action by using the unused space in your sales letter.

What unused space?

Most people don't print on the reverse side of their letter! Blank space doesn't sell! When you can incorporate copy on the reverse side of your letter you are giving yourself one more opportunity to convert that prospect into a customer. One of the most effective methods of copy to use on the reverse side of your sales letter is that of testimonials.

Testimonials on the reverse side of your sales letter provide you with the following benefits:

1. They let the prospect know others have tried your service before
2. They provide you with another opportunity to make a call to action
3. They demonstrate 3rd party verification
4. They let you share more of your marketing message (Hint: testimonials should share key parts of your service and how you are different)

By combining the power of testimonials with your sales letter you can get more phone calls every time your letters go out. For maximum impact gather testimonials (and put them on your website too) that speak specifically to your core offering. The more specific (i.e. a testimonial that says "I was doubtful when I first got a letter in the mail...") your testimonials the more they help your letter.

Discover how you can use sales letters, website marketing, social networking and more as part of a marketing system that will get you to a 7 figure NET income by calling me directly at 303-841-8008.

Does Your Marketing Plan Account for Failure?

When entrepreneurs start a new business or even a new division of an existing business they often spend a good deal of time on their marketing plan. Often they spend too much time on planning trying to analyze every item that should be done to ensure the business is a raging success. Some marketing plans go into excruciating detail of the specific actions that should be done.

One of the items that are usually missing from most marketing plans is the simple part of accounting for failure. I am not suggesting that the entire business will be a failure, but accounting for a part of your plan not to reach the expected results.

Consider the following item that is often part of most marketing plans.

- Create a lead generating website by X date

While this is a simple line item on most marketing plans; consider asking yourself the following questions:

- What happens when the website doesn't get done on time?
- How soon will leads start pouring in?
- What will I do if leads don't start pouring in?
- How long will I give the website to work before I make a change?

These are just a few of the questions to ask on that single action item! To get your marketing working often takes time and testing. While you might not want to call it a "failure" when a website doesn't generate leads from day one, to ensure your business survives consider having alternate solutions as you create your plan.

To get the most out of your marketing plan, consider identifying key alternatives for each action item (each marketing system should have methods of testing). It doesn't have to be complex (and really shouldn't be) but consider the following items as part of your overall plan and strategy.

- **Time** – Identify time for each item. Time to put the marketing piece into action, time to allow it to work, and time related to making changes/tweaks. By allowing yourself a defined period of time you won't stick with something that isn't working too long and you will also give it time to succeed.
- **Cost** – What is a customer worth to your business? When you can answer this question it will help you to decide what you can invest in each marketing system. While investing in your business is important you don't want to invest an amount that can cause you to have a 10 year ROI.

When you put a marketing plan into action, allow yourself time for testing. Testing can prevent you from giving up too soon on a system or even your business.

About The Authors

About Todd Bates

As a pioneer in the marketing field Todd has created 47 different companies that have helped small businesses put strategies into action that quickly increase their sales. He is well known for his ability to get attendees to overcome their fears to take their business to the next level. Specializing in direct response marketing, sales conversion methods, and social marketing strategies, Todd has a passion for helping individuals and business improve their bottom line.

Todd's direct and "over the top" style in speaking brings audiences to life and prepares them to take action. Attendees laugh as they discover his methods and feel like they are the only one in the room. By the end they have clear action items that they can take home to improve their sales. Todd's philosophy of overcoming fears, focusing on key money making activities, and taking action gives attendees no room for failure.

Since 1990 Todd has been sharing his strategies with individuals and small business owners. He has shared his methods and techniques with over 250,000 people through his speaking events. A dedication to helping people in his unique 1 on 1 style has allowed him to help over 15,000 individual business owners. As markets and business needs change he continues to adapt sharing new methods to keep his clients performing with a focus on generating a high net income.

About James & Joey Bridges

With a background in IT that started from their days at the University of Southern California James and Joey have been developing Internet based solutions for over 14 years.

As consultants to major Fortune 500 companies they developed web based systems that increased productivity and profitability. The systems they developed were used by small departments and those with user bases in excess of 50,000.

During their time as consultants they taught as Instructors in the Internet Technology Program at the University of Southern California for 6 years instructing students and staff on how to implement web technologies. Both James and Joseph hold the certifications as Google Adwords Qualified Individuals.

Starting in 2003 they created a real estate company that sold over 100 million in real estate from the Internet. This company continues to operate today without the daily management of James and Joseph.

Since 2007 James and Joseph have launched additional online businesses and in 2009 built a 7 figure coaching and training business in 7 months.

Assisting small business owners and entrepreneurs generate sales from Facebook has been their passion since late 2007. They have developed models that they share while speaking and training across the United States for business owners to grow their sales through the use of social media on Facebook.

A Special FREE Gift from the Author

To Help You Get The Most Out Of This Book There is a Collection of

FREE Extra Resources Waiting For you at:

www.ToddBatesBook.com/Resources

Just a few of the resources that are waiting for you are listed below plus additional ones that we don't even have space to mention.

- ✓ Complete audio training course done by the author to help you overcome your E.I.D.
- ✓ E.I.D checklists to use daily to reach your goals and avoid tasks that waste your time, energy, and effort.
- ✓ Todd Bates exclusive marketing manifesto report to immediately generate sales for your business.
- ✓ Special reader certificate that entitles you to speak directly with the author.
- ✓ 10 strategies to finding your niche & dominating it in 16 months
- ✓ 10 Questions to generate sales now.

Todd Bates Speaking & Training Offerings

Live Custom Training For Your Group or Meeting That Delivers Immediate Items To Generate Increased Sales

Call For Info: 303-841-8008

From keynote addresses to intimate gatherings Todd & his team will deliver a custom message to your audience.

- ✓ Every attendee of your meeting receives their own copy of Todd's latest book

- ✓ Todd and his team of speakers can come to your group from 50 to 500 and deliver content that fits your requirements.

- ✓ Topics range from Marketing to Social Media training to Sales Conversion.

- ✓ Every attendee receives a coaching coupon to speak with Todd or one of his trained coaches ($395 value).

- ✓ Every attendee receives Todd's 11 Rules for Business Success CD ($97 value).

Todd Bates FREE Audio Training with Weekly Podcast

Weekly Todd delivers audo training to guide you to success in your business

Join his podcast by visiting iTunes and type in "Todd Bates"

Each weekly training Todd provides the following help to get your business to the next level

- ✓ Step by step help so you can immediately take action after the call.

- ✓ Access to resources, materials, and information only available for attendees of the weekly training.

- ✓ Time to get your specific questions answered through Todd's Q&A.

- ✓ Topics range from Marketing to Social Media training to Sales Conversion.

www.ingramcontent.com/pod-product-compliance
Lightning Source LLC
Chambersburg PA
CBHW031052180526
45163CB00002BA/807